# European History

Everything You Need to Know to Ace Saq

*(Explore the Astonishing Rebirth of European History From Beginning to End)*

**Robert Mackey**

Published By **Kate Sanders**

# Robert Mackey

All Rights Reserved

*European History: Everything You Need to Know to Ace Saq (Explore the Astonishing Rebirth of European History From Beginning to End)*

# ISBN 978-0-9949563-3-0

No part of this guidebook shall be reproduced in any form without permission in writing from the publisher except in the case of brief quotations embodied in critical articles or reviews.

Legal & Disclaimer

The information contained in this book is not designed to replace or take the place of any form of medicine or professional medical advice. The information in this book has been provided for educational & entertainment purposes only.

The information contained in this book has been compiled from sources deemed reliable, and it is accurate to the best of the Author's knowledge; however, the Author cannot guarantee its accuracy and validity and cannot be held liable for any errors or omissions. Changes are periodically made to this book. You must consult your doctor or get professional medical advice before using any of the suggested remedies, techniques, or information in this book.

Upon using the information contained in this book, you agree to hold harmless the Author from and against any damages, costs, and expenses, including any legal fees potentially resulting from the application of any of the information provided by this guide. This disclaimer applies to any damages or injury caused by the use and application, whether directly or indirectly, of any advice or information presented, whether for breach of contract, tort, negligence, personal injury, criminal intent, or under any other cause of action.

You agree to accept all risks of using the information presented inside this book. You need to consult a professional medical practitioner in order to ensure you are both able and healthy enough to participate in this program.

## Table Of Contents

Chapter 1: Setting the Tone for the Renaissance ............... 1

Chapter 2: Great Artists and Art of the Renaissance ............................. 26

Chapter 3: Renaissance Entertainment ... 47

Chapter 4: Great Scientists and Discoveries during the Renaissance ........................... 58

Chapter 5: Important Figures of the Renaissance ................................. 73

Chapter 6: The Beleaguered Backdrop ... 87

Chapter 7: The Medici Funding Of the Renaissance ........................................... 106

Chapter 8: Wolves of the Renaissance .. 123

Chapter 9: Art Leonardo Da Vinci .......... 133

Chapter 10: Michelangelo ..................... 146

Chapter 11: Hans Holbein ..................... 162

Chapter 12: Architects And Engineers .. 174

Chapter 13: Writer And Architect ......... 180

## Chapter 1: Setting the Tone for the Renaissance

The early years of the Renaissance set the quantity for the crucial turning point it is probably for civilization. It bridged the gap amongst current-day-day civilization and the Middle Ages, being duration of rebirth for maximum of humanity, and changed into rich in artwork, tune, and the sciences. Many super thinkers and philosophers emerged all through the time, and worldwide exploration have turn out to be at its pinnacle, inviting the lifestyle of recent lands to European change.

Though the Middle Ages had been taken into consideration a darker time, historians typically agree payments are exaggerated, however had a few improvements in technological know-how and art work. The fall of the Roman Empire additionally left many human beings suffering with war, famine, and plagues like the Black Death that unfold throughout Europe. Times had been difficult, but similarly they created the correct situations for the imminent Renaissance length.

The Renaissance revived more than just classical literature and art office work. The tone for the Renaissance changed into set through popularity of change. The mind of the time advocated people to discover, each their very personal talents and the world round them, that have turn out to be a far cry from the lives human beings professional at some point of the medieval times. As the Renaissance persisted so did the severa adjustments. This economic disaster will skip over a number of the strategies social shape, faith, human perception, and shape modified inside the Renaissance length. We'll moreover communicate the geography of the

Renaissance. These factors and modifications all worked collectively to make the Renaissance the terrific length in human statistics it might become.

## The Early Renaissance: Florence, Italy

### Florence

The Medici own family lived and dominated in Florence, Italy, for six decades at the start of the Renaissance duration. They have been heavy supporters of the humanist movements, that is one purpose humans preserve in mind Florence because the birthplace of the Renaissance. Though there was a famend interest in growing artwork, it changed into no longer however a worthwhile mission. Florence, however, had each many wealthy citizens who had the finances to help new artists and their ventures further to a wealthy cultural records best for idea.

The thoughts that sparked the Renaissance unfold first to surrounding Italian metropolis-states, which include Bologna, Rome, Venice, Ferrara, and Milan. The ideas did no longer spread to France till the fifteenth century, and then to northern and western Europe. The beginning of the Renaissance period changed into exceptional for each of the international locations in the course of Europe.

At the time of the Renaissance, the Italian City-States had come out of financial melancholy and professional an monetary growth as a end result. This growth granted those metropolis-states greater wealth and electricity than unique towns in Europe. However, each of the city-states have end up governed one after the other, with a few having elected leaders and others being dominated thru a monarchy. These cities often fought each wonderful over belongings and territory. Some of the greater important city-states included:

Florence- As the birthplace of the Renaissance, this town-u.S.A. Of the united states modified into one of the wealthiest, boasting early architectural achievements and have become a famous preference among artists seeking out paintings on the time. The Medici circle of relatives ruled until it have grow to be a democracy. Florence end up also seemed for being a banking center and for its fabric manufacturing.

Rome- The pope dominated over the Roman metropolis-state and the Catholic Church on the start of the 1400s. In 1447, Nicholas V started out re-constructing Rome. Under his management, Rome started out assisting the arts. Michelangelo and Raphael are every famous for his or her art work performed right right here, mainly on the ceiling of the Sistine Chapel and the improvement of St. Peter's Basilica.

Milan- Milan did not grow to be wealthy till later in the 1400s as it have become in the Middle Age time period till 1450 while the Sforza circle of relatives dominated. With a current day peace with Florence furthermore came a more hobby in the thoughts of the Renaissance. Eventually, Milan have become famous for its metalwork, such as weapons and suits of armor.

Naples- Naples controlled most of the southern part of Italy within the direction of the Renaissance and turned into one of the later cities to embody the Renaissance. The motion took keep in 1443 even as Alfonso I conquered the city. It persevered to be a consumer of the arts, turning into famous for the discovery of the mandolin and the tune produced at the time. Spain conquered Naples in 1504.

A small metropolis-country named Ferrara modified into moreover regarded for song and theatre.

Venice- The island city of Venice received its wealth and reputation with the useful resource of trading with the Far East, bringing silk and spices returned to Italy. Its characteristic took a temporary decline even as the Ottoman Empire conquered Constantinople. However, it maintained manage over the seas east of Italy. Venice is also recognized for its manufacturing of inventive glassware.

Though the town-states did combat among themselves, an eventual peace have become treaty signed in 1454. Milan, Naples, and Florence signed The Peace of Lodi. With limitations in region, the treaty saved matters non violent for 3 a long time.

The Renaissance as a Rebirth

The Renaissance have end up a rebirth of the information, attitudes, and classical reading from the Ancient Greek and Roman instances. People studied classical texts and strategies, regularly with the intention of improving their non-public conditions. An early founder pupil and poet inside the Renaissance, a person named Petrarch is the numerous ones credited for uplifting this gaining knowledge of. He had a ardour for attempting to find and know-how the historic texts, insistent that records the available manuscripts could result in civilizing thoughts.

Though people bear in mind the Renaissance a motion of cultural and intellectual proportions, it became moreover carefully related to politics, society, and discovery. While older practices and idea had been brought decrease lower back to lifestyles, those moreover spurred dynamic trade. Explorers favored new continents, decided new trade routes, and created extra connections with the area.

While this changed into the maximum terrific Renaissance, it grow to be now not the best Renaissance in European records. The Carolingian Renaissance happened from the eighth to ninth centuries, and the Twelfth Century Renaissance noticed the return of Greek philosophy and technological facts. Every Renaissance become a rebirth of classical life-style and idea. Though way of existence and perception had never disappeared in reality, the Renaissance added them to the leading part over again.

Social Culture of the Early Renaissance

Wealth and standing had been intently answerable for an character's route in life. Prior to the Renaissance, the Black Death had killed masses of heaps. Those who had survived had get right of entry to to the same assets, and many humans rose inside the social scores as a cease give up result. Fortunately for artists and students of the time, people used wealth and life-style to boost their statuses in society. By supporting those artists and students, the newfound wealth of many Europeans funded the cultural revolution.

Even no matter the reality that the Renaissance unfold from u.S. Of america to u.S.A., the today's arts and mind were comparable however precise to one among a type regions. Often, Renaissance thoughts tied into the manner of life of the location. However, they also tied into the middle of this period of rebirth and the functionality it had for trade. It regularly unfold via the lessons of students and diplomats, shared among artists, via marriage, trade, and even military invasions. As the Renaissance modified into some aspect that unfold from a number one issue, each territory had its very own Renaissance period.

Historians regularly disagree about the forestall of the Renaissance, with a few saying it ended in the 1520s and others announcing it ended within the 1620s. This confrontation comes from the spread of the Renaissance, as many European nations professional it throughout unique time durations. It additionally unfold past the borders of Europe and inspired cultures across the arena. As it passed off at such a lot of precise instances in specific regions, the Renaissance is on occasion damaged into geographical groups, which include the Italian Renaissance, the English Renaissance, and the Northern Renaissance. It moreover improved to the east, Africa, and the Americas.

Religion in the Early Renaissance

The Black Death that had killed hundreds of loads left many Europeans in worry of an angry, vengeful God. The Black Death reached Europe in the 1350s. People had been shocked at the equal time as large ships carried useless or near-dead sailors into port. Many humans anticipated to appearance their own family all yet again, but, they'll find that their circle of relatives individuals had been deceased or had fallen unwell.

Some human beings isolated themselves from the ones own family individuals, while others attempted their nice to take care of them. Those infected with the Black Death rarely recovered. The situation changed into worse because of the individual of the illness. It have come to be airborne, which supposed that someone reduced in size the ailment through breathing in infected air.

The negative response to the Black Death become brought approximately by means of the use of a lack of expertise approximately the man or woman of the illness. People did now not apprehend the way it unfold and believed God modified into punishing them. Because of this fear, humans of decrease social reputation, wrongdoers, and slaves were often crushed. This form of sacrifice confirmed the vengeful God that people believed humankind changed into repenting for its sins.

Though the beatings had no longer whatever to do with its eradication, the Black Death in the end died out. Europe have become one of the remaining areas inflamed. Looking at the response to the Black Death, the shift in thoughts-set following its eradication marked a number one milestone for the Renaissance period. Humanism played a tremendous trouble on this shift some distance from religion. Humanism, with the aid of using definition, is a focus on the human in preference to a deity. This shift did not really get rid of religion—it have become though distinguished in lots of human beings's lives. However, people started to question their very non-public existences and capabilities in a way that led them to separate themselves from religion and have fun their very non-public strengths. Through embracing these ideas, humanism modified how humans checked out religion of their lives. They were not much less moral or ethical in any way. If a few aspect, human beings had general extra responsibility for selecting their lives and choices.

Early in the Renaissance, the Catholic Church become perfect. Christianity have become the principle faith, and those who did now not exercise it were often outcasts. However, the Renaissance delivered about a alternate. In addition to the thoughts of humanism, the Catholic Church confronted demanding situations from Protestantism. Though Protestantism became a form of Christianity, it although challenged a number of the Catholic ideas of the time.

Architecture inside the Renaissance

During the Medieval times, people positioned a good buy of interest on religion and political shape. Much of the form attributed to that factor is Gothic-fashion castles and church buildings. These have a more 'rectangular-like' layout in the direction of the pinnacle and function even strains.

During the Renaissance, but, architecture changed to reflect the forms of Ancient Rome and Greece. Some features of Renaissance houses protected:

Square layout not unusual- Though the tops of houses have been rounded, homes as an entire have been constructed from rectangle or rectangular symmetrical shapes.

Front- The 'façade,' or front, of homes additionally had symmetry, typically at some point of a vertical axis, which means the left issue changed into similar to the right.

Columns- Columns used at some stage in the Renaissance period are much like the ones used within the route of the instances of the Roman empire.

Domes and Arches- Greek and Roman shape inspired the rounded layout of building tops.

Ceilings- During the Middle Ages, ceilings every now and then had been left completely open. Renaissance builders commonly created flat ceilings, with the exception being the domed regions of houses.

Though many architectural designs have been borrowed from the Greeks and Romans, the person credited with bringing them to existence changed into Filippo Brunelleschi. Considered the first Renaissance architect, Brunelleschi began out out his first piece of Renaissance form in 1419 even as he designed the dome that stands above the cathedral of Florence. Many historians additionally keep in mind this 365 days as the very begin of the Renaissance length.

People remember The Pantheon in Ancient Rome as the biggest dome shape, constructed 1500 years before Brunelleschi's paintings on the cathedral of Florence. The cathedral's dome have become a first rate piece for its length. This venture may also want to take Brunelleschi lots of his life to complete.

Four million bricks make up the dome, and the gold ball that sits on pinnacle weighs almost tons. To assemble this, Brunelleschi needed to provide you with procedures to raise the heavy objects immoderate into the air. Other homes he designed encompass the church buildings of Santo Spirito and San Lorenzo.

Many different European church homes were designed in a comparable fashion. Some other houses that have a real Renaissance architectural format encompass El Escorial, The Sistine Chapel, Basilica of St. Peter, Palazzo Farnese, Pazzi Chapel, and Palazzo Pitti.

The Life of the Average Person at some stage in the Renaissance

In the Middle Ages, the ones of excessive social popularity or royalty have been more likely to enjoy the luxuries of existence. The commonplace person, or 'peasant,' can also have struggled to discover meals. Even farmers and people who processed items regularly had problem taking part in the end bring about their labors, as those of better social popularity taxed gadgets or took them for his or her very personal. While the lifestyles of the not unusual peasant or farmer did no longer alternate considerably with the Renaissance, they were capable of live with no hassle. They had been capable of eat and hold their existence. However, most nevertheless labored from sun as an entire lot as sun down. The commonplace bad farmer lived in a single-room hut together together with his family. The commonplace character survived on bread and stew crafted from a few factor emerge as to be had at the time, generally greens or eggs. When feasible, the terrible may additionally drink wine or beer with their food. Water changed into not sanitized, so ingesting it can cause infection.

Farmers and peasants not often ate meat. Those close to the coast need to take gain in their vicinity through fishing, however most meat changed into pricey and hard to return back via using way of. There turn out to be no refrigeration then, so people used salt to maintain meat. As salt changed into uncommon, preserved meats had been highly-priced. In addition to stew and bread, human beings may eat mush, typically oats or wheat soaked in water to melt.

The Lifestyle of the Middle Class

Some peasants and farmers secured a higher social reputation within the Renaissance. Those with sufficient wealth to be considered center-elegance citizens lived in bigger houses. Compared to the dwelling fashion that most human beings are used to nowadays, those houses had been darkish and bloodless. The loss of hygiene at the time supposed they were probably smelly, too. Technology had no longer but advanced sufficient to allow human beings to have walking water or indoor lavatories. However, middle splendor had get proper of access to to many luxuries. Women wore prolonged, fancy robes on the equal time as men commonly wore pants with an excellent coat known as a doublet.

The rich had get entry to to food better than truely bread and stew. Often, the rich hosted big feasts with many unusual dishes. Though in addition they ate stew and broth, individual spices or sugar, secured via change, flavored the food of the rich. Large roasts of pig beef or stag have been organized by using using the usage of boiling and basting with rose water and the juices of the meats. They also ate large pastime birds, at the side of cranes, peacocks, and swans on specific sports activities like gala's or weddings. Once the birds have been cooked, people used the feathers as decoration. Mutton, pheasant, ham, turkey, chook, rabbit, and venison had been additionally commonly eaten. Dessert changed right into a 'fruit path' that consisted of jellies, fruit, cheese, and nuts.

Children During the Renaissance

The existence you stay these days is probably enormously wonderful from the lives of youngsters within the Renaissance. Adults anticipated youngsters to act maturely. Once children have been vintage enough, they spoke, acted, and dressed like adults. Most youngsters started out working as quick as they were in a role. Unfortunately, many youngsters grew up feeling unloved via their parents. They labored lengthy hours and did no longer have time for play. Additionally, maximum kids were not coddled, hugged, or in any other case shown love.

The Renaissance length did result in a change for children of wealthier households. Children of households with more reputation had more free time. They need to experience their children and accomplished in desire to worked. Once those wealthier children were older, person men have been normally sent to college or had a private teach. Arithmetic and grammar have been a heavy recognition. After humanism grow to be brought, some studied public talking, philosophy, and Latin.

Government During the Renaissance

During the Renaissance, many regions of life underwent radical modifications. For many governments, however, the equal absolute monarchy device existed because it did in the direction of the Middle Ages. Having a single ruler made matters much much less hard all through this time. However, conflict was tons less of a focus in some unspecified time in the future of the Renaissance. Eventually, a few areas even evolved to useful resource a democracy.

Florence, Italy, end up one vicinity that supported democracy. Wealthy households ruled according with what the human beings wanted on the time. However, many others ruled with none constraints. Queen Isabella I and her husband Ferdinand II dominated over Spain, and their phrase became regulation. Their fantastic-grandson, Philip II, come to be one of the first in Spain to face struggles, as opposing sports rose up to venture his criminal recommendations.

England had a exceptional machine, with Elizabeth I ruling alongside a parliament.

Even with the parliament, Elizabeth made maximum of the choices. In Germany, the Holy Roman Empire however dominated. This setup complex subjects, as there has been a unmarried emperor on the pinnacle who dominated with seven elected officers, many princes, and leaders of the eighty imperial unfastened towns the Holy Roman Empire managed.

## Chapter 2: Great Artists and Art of the Renaissance

We understand approximately many amazing Renaissance artists nowadays. Some experienced reputation in their lifetime, even as others could not come to be well-known until they had surpassed, and their artwork modified into located centuries later. Many paintings and sculptures from this term can be visible in museums internationally. The data available on plenty of these artists comes from the e book, Lives of the Most Eminent Painters, Sculptors, & Architects through Giorgio Vasari. He changed into inside the social circle of loads of these artists, despite the fact that he by no means completed repute as an artist himself. Published in 1568, the e-book documented the lives and works of many later Renaissance artists. The special information to be had has been pieced collectively from to be had files and surviving paintings from the time.

Donatello (Donato di Niccolo di Betto Bardi)

Born in Florence in 1386, Donatello come to be one of the older Renaissance painters and had close to ties to the Medici family. Donatello in all likelihood received his earliest training from a nearby goldsmith. He started apprenticing under sculptor and metal smith, Lorenzo Ghiberti, in 1403. Donatello furthermore worked closely with Ghiberti in growing the bronze doors at the Baptistery of the Florence Cathedral.

Sometime round 1407, Donatello became pals with once rival-artist Filippo Brunelleschi. They traveled to Rome collectively, and the 2 can also have studied the ruins of classical Rome. These classical impacts and Brunelleschi's Gothic fashion are apparent in a number of Donatello's in advance quantities.

## Donatello's Art

Following the gaining knowledge of duration of his life, Donatello went right away to create many portions of artwork. His rendition of the David became a existence-duration statue carved from marble. The Gothic style he discovered out is apparent within the expressionless face and long, glossy traces. This style have emerge as quite impassive in assessment to Donatello's later paintings.

Donatello labored with Italian architect and sculptor Michelozzo spherical 1425. As each had studied alongside Lorenzo Ghiberti, the pair worked properly collectively. They were commissioned to create severa architectural-sculptural tombs. Their paintings could in all likelihood encourage many future

Florentine burial chambers. Among the tombs they created had been the ones for Cardinal Brancacci and Antipope John XXII.

Donatello's 2d depiction of David changed into lots more well-known than his first. This sculpture became commissioned by means of way of way of Cosimo de Medici. This time, the sculpture have become constructed from bronze and stands free of any architectural surroundings. The message sent with the aid of way of David is one of the triumph of civic certainly one of a kind feature over irrationality and brutality, which aligned cautiously with the beliefs of the time.

Another of Donatello's well-known bronze statues became Gattamelata. Created in Padua, mercenary Erasmo da Narni commissioned this piece.. The statue suggests the mercenary the usage of a horse, dressed as though he had been equipped for warfare. This piece became extraordinarily arguable at the time as fine kings and rulers had been depicted on equestrian statues. Despite its arguable nature, the statue went right away to inspire many others that observed.

Crucifixion emerge as some exclusive of Donatello's top notch quantities. Though it become a bronze alleviation sculpture, it mimicked a painting with its depiction of a scene and interest to detail. It was made using bronze, gold, and silver round 1465. Its specific layout creates a play of slight and darkness with the shadows throughout the surface of the sculpture.

Sandro Botticelli (Alessandro di Mariano Filipepi)

Botticelli became born in 1455 in Florence. Though he became born early in the Renaissance, his portray style in his works which include the Primavera and The Birth of Venus capture the actual Renaissance spirit. He modified into named Botticelli, or 'little barrel' after a nickname given to his brother who worked as a pawnbroker. He become specially expert within the arts of fresco and panel portray. His linear attitude moreover allowed him to advantage a feel of human symmetry and perfection in his works, which is specifically easy in The Birth of Venus.

Botticelli studied underneath Filippo Lippi, one of the most official Florentine masters whose fashion become lots softer and similarly sensitive than what Botticelli's style could probably grow to be, for several years. While Filippo Lippi's affects can be actually visible in Botticelli's preference of paler solar sun shades and touchy, fanciful get dressed, the student developed more potent strains and extra resonant colour schemes.

In addition to what he positioned out from Lippi, Botticelli also studied the sculptural factors beneath Andrea del Verrocchio and Antonio Pollaiuolo, high-quality painters. In 1482, he contributed to the Sistine Chapel.

Botticelli's Art

Botticelli painted The Birth of Venus, commissioned through Medici, in 1485. Though Venus is taken into consideration a mythological goddess, the idea became to depict a completely unique event instead of to inform a mythological story. It is part of a fixed, with the paintings Primavera, Pallas, and Venus and Mars.

Botticelli created Virgin and Child with an Angel ultimately earlier than 1740. In this photograph, Botticelli suggests a mom and little one embracing with an angel close by. This artwork is considered considered certainly one of numerous with the resource of Botticelli with a similar style. There is a portray of the Virgin Mary and her baby with out an angel, in addition to a version with angels in area of 1.

Hieronymus Bosch

Hieronymus Bosch is known as being one of the crucial artists from outside Italy that observed a humanist technique. He end up maximum well-known within the international locations of the Netherlands, Spain, and Austria. Bosch lived from 1450 to 1516, and he likely discovered to color from his circle of relatives, as his father have become an imaginative adviser and his grandfather and uncles worked as artists.

Bosch's most famous portray is The Garden of Earthly Delights, which historians believe became created amongst 1495 and 1505. This precise piece is a triptych, that is a painting with three panels hinged together. On the left, God is introducing Adam and Eve to the Garden of Eden. The middle panel displays the enticements of society, and the proper panel depicts Judgment Day. Art scholars accept as true with the underlying mission of this piece may additionally have been the risks of temptation.

Leonardo da Vinci

Da Vinci is arguably one of the most famous artists from the Renaissance. He is less-identified for his enhancements but have come to be a very well-known painter. Da Vinci end up born in 1452 and studied art work for 4 years from 1466 starting as an apprentice. It took him some years to reveal off his abilities, however he commenced out accepting commissions in 1478. Da Vinci's artwork obligations of the time ranged from designing monuments to helping with parade floats.

Regarding his artwork, there are first-class about 15 of his artwork that still continue to exist. There had been many portions that da Vinci did not prevent earlier than his lack of existence in 1519, as he often tried new techniques (and without success). Da Vinci come to be moreover identified for his procrastinating thoughts-set, specifically because he studied such a variety of fields. However, the drawings, thoughts, and scientific diagrams in his sketchbooks may go straight away to make a contribution to many incredible fields.

Da Vinci's Art

Though the Mona Lisa depicts what looks as if a woman, some historians believe that it may had been a self-portrait of da Vinci. Other theories are that the Mona Lisa have become a portrait of a citizen's partner. Da Vinci painted the Mona Lisa amongst 1503 and 1506. Today, you could see it in Paris, France, on the Louvre Museum.

The Last Supper is an iconic painting of Jesus and his twelve disciples, on the time whilst Jesus knew that one must betray him. This painting come to be a mural built among 1495 and 1497 that covers a monastery wall in Milan, Italy. However, due to the way da Vinci experimented with oil and tempera paint on the drywall, the current-day mural is often a reconstruction that has been maintained and restored through the years.

Vitruvian Man is a painting of someone superimposed in positions. It is referred to as after the architect Vitruvius. People receive as actual with da Vinci created it in 1490. The drawing is placed in Venice, Italy on the Gallerie dell'Academia, however, it is not in reality displayed.

Albrecht Durer

Born in 1471 in the metropolis of Nurnberg, Germany, Durer is one of the most influential artist of the German Renaissance. Many of his art work portions had been religious in nature. He had a Gothic fashion apparent in his in advance art work and end up maximum widely recognized for his spiritual works, altarpieces, and copper engravings. He moreover did numerous pics and self-pix, in addition to woodcuts.

Before he changed into professional as a painter, Durer worked in his father's goldsmith workshop. However, he turn out to be best thirteen whilst he completed his first self-portrait and 14 whilst he finished the painting Madonna with Musical Angels. Recognizing his obvious understanding, his father secured Durer an apprenticeship with Michael Wohlgemuth, a woodcut illustrator and painter of the time.

Durer could go to Italy for the primary time round 1494. Here, he placed many new painting strategies from the Renaissance artists of the time, which may be obvious in his later works. Some of his early affects encompass Andrea Mantegna, Antonio Pollaiuolo, and Giovanni Bellini.

One of the ultimate and pleasant portray Durer created modified into The Four Apostles. Completed in 1526, the portray depicts Saints John, Peter, Paul, and Mark. Artists have a superb time his work as some of the most lovable quantities of paintings across the European continent. Durer may want to have an effect on Dutch, Italian, German, and outstanding artists.

Michelangelo Buonarroti

Though this iconic artist have become born in Caprese, Italy in 1475, he grew up in Florence. Michelangelo holds the titles of painter, sculptor, and architect. He were given his begin younger, being invited to stay at the palace of Lorenzo de' Medici and commenced his apprenticeship at age thirteen-14. He labored with many people in Medici's social circle and became in the end commissioned with the aid of the usage of many terrific works at a few diploma in the Renaissance, together with a cathedral, a cardinal, and the pope.

Michelangelo is one of the maximum well-documented artists of his time. While others need to collect later popularity, he changed into in immoderate name for within the path of his lifetime. Many of his portions depicted perfectionism and great hobby to detail. While Michelangelo insisted his thoughts had been his very very own and that he created art work with out outdoor have an effect on, some of his Madonna portions display apparent have an effect on from the art work of Leonardo da Vinci.

Michelangelo's Art

David symbolizes the proper of human perfection in some unspecified time in the future of the Renaissance. Incredible hobby to element went into this statue, which stands 17-toes tall. The David changed into commissioned in 1501 and became modeled after the biblical hero.

The Pope commissioned the ceiling of the Sistine Chapel in 1508, and it took Michelangelo 4 years to complete. While Michelangelo have end up in the starting paid to depict the twelve apostles, he painted nine scenes from the Book of Genesis inside the Bible. Within those nine scenes, there were seven male prophets and five girl prophets. The most famous scene depicted come to be The Creation of Adam, a piece wherein God reaches out to Adam and they touch fingers.

Michelangelo had many specific well-known art work portions in his time that can be located all round Europe. They are dispersed due to the fact, like many different artists, he sought out artwork in towns beyond Italy, in particular following the fall of the Medici family in 1494. Some of his portions encompass:

The Tomb and Shrine of St. Dominic- Michelangelo finished this piece in Bologna. It end up the art work via using a deceased sculptor that had now not been finished. Michelangelo carved the closing of the small figures that finished the tomb and shrine. His three figures stood out more than the preceding sculptures because of his interest to element.

The Bacchus- Designed among 1496 and 1497, the Bacchus is considered one of Michelangelo's first sculptures, depicting the Roman God of Wine, Bacchus. The pose of Bacchus indicates drunkenness depicted via a high-quality body and rolling eyes.

The Pietà- The Pieta is the great sculpture Michelangelo ever signed. It was created amongst 1498 and 1499 the usage of Carrara marble. In this artwork, the frame of Jesus is lying for the duration of his mom's, Mary, lap following the crucifixion. It changed into on the begin created for Cardinal Jean de Bilheres' funeral and modified into later moved to St. Peter's Basilica.

Raphael (Raffaello Santi)

Though Raphael only lived 37 years, his classical painting strategies may hold to steer artists nicely into the middle of the 19th century. He turn out to be impacts by means of manner of arts via manner of Uccello, Mantegna, Piero Della Francesca, and Perugino, even though he likely received schooling from his father, who turn out to be a court docket painter, as properly. Raphael have become born in 1483 and have emerge as maximum well-known at some point of his lifetime for developing pix and art work of Madonnas.

Raphael's well connections have been furthermore advanced with the resource of his family's wealth. He served as an apprentice under Pietro Perugino for 4 years starting in 1500. Raphael would skip right away to be commissioned for lots paintings in his lifetime, as his high social popularity gave him connections to the folks who may pay for his artwork.

While his social circle attracted people who praised Raphael's extremely good works, it additionally attracted enemies. Raphael is taken into consideration one of the maximum severa painters of the Renaissance length because of the truth he changed into pretty proficient at absorbing and studying the styles of the ones round him. There had been obvious affects from exclusive artists, and Raphael had taken to the ones styles obviously. Michelangelo even accused him of plagiarism, although his accusations have been never proved.

Raphael's Art

The Sistine Madonna is one in each of Raphael's maximum analyzed portions. The way it's far painted shows easy have an effect on from Perugino. Painted inside the early 1500s, the Madonna also can additionally have been an define of Raphael's mistress, who he have emerge as with from 1508 until his death in 1520.

Saint George and the Dragon is one of portions thru Raphael with a similar subject remember. It turn out to be a painting indoors a sequence of mini panels that changed into painted in Florence in party for the court of Urbino. The portray informed the tale of Saint George, a Roman soldier of Christian faith. He killed a dragon that had determined the daughter of a pagan king right into a city, which then precipitated the king and all folks who observed him to become Christians.

Raphael moved to work in the Vatican in Rome in 1508 and Pope Julius II commissioned Raphael to paint his personal library. Here, Raphael completed particular works which have been commissioned thru a predecessor. As an entire, the paintings achieved in the library is called Stanza della Segnatura. Several individual portions were painted on every of the walls, along with The Disputation of the Holy Sacrament, The School of Athens, and Parnassus.

Titian (Tiziano Vecelli)

Historians argue the date of Titian's transport even though it is formally recorded as 1477. Many historians consider Titian have become born within the mountain village of Pieve di Cadore on a mountaintop in Italy among 1488 and 1490. He received his education at the Venetian School of Art, and is taken into consideration the finest Renaissance painter who graduated from right here. His fantastic hobby to emotion and the idea of human perfection are depicted sooner or later of his artwork. Titian may want to have his works recreated by using way of famous masters like Nicolas Poussin and Rubens, who complimented him of their imitation of his fashion.

## Chapter 3: Renaissance Entertainment

The Renaissance period had masses extra middle-beauty citizens than the middle Ages did. These human beings did now not should toil all day and night time as farmers and peasants formerly did to earn a residing and hold their existence leaving masses of time for entertainment. Entertainment at a few stage within the Renaissance length blanketed tune, dancing, and theatre. The invention of the printing press allowed people greater get right of access to to song and performs than earlier than because of the reality composers ought to percentage their mind with those who knew a way to play gadgets. Several musical devices had been moreover invented and used at a few stage in the Renaissance duration, which includes the violin.

Music and Dance

Music and dance have been some of the great kinds of leisure, as they did now not cost something. Even farmers and peasants may also want to sing and dance for amusement As the Renaissance continued, humans commenced out learning new combos of voices and a way to play gadgets. Many famous composers also lived within the route of this time, including Thomas Tallis, Josquin Des Prez, and William Byrd. In 1607, Claudio Monteverdi wrote the primary dramatic opera.

Vocal Music

One famous shape of music at the time became choir music. It have emerge as well-known inside the church, in which one-of-a-kind vocals and voice kinds were woven together to supply a totally specific melodious harmony. The interweaving technique have become known as polyphony. Madrigal, a form of vocal tune that had at the least three-6 singers, moreover have emerge as famous. Several melodies have been sung at once to create a more revel in of emotion. Romantic poems have been commonly sung as madrigal tune.

Instruments

Creating track with devices have become no longer a trendy concept. However, many gadgets had been improved upon within the Renaissance period. The first violin became additionally made at some stage in the Renaissance, inside the early 1500s. In addition to woodwind devices like the recorder and bagpipe, a few famous options embody:

Hurdy Gurdy- This tool had a comparable form to a violin. Instead of a bow, a small keyboard is used. Each key corresponds to a string. When the secret's completed, a wheel rubs in competition to the string and makes a sound.

Hurdy Gurdy

Lute- The lute is just like a guitar however has a rounded lower decrease lower back. People might in all likelihood pluck those strings to make song instead of strumming them.

Harpsichord- This tool is just like a piano, but it's miles plucked in area of hit.

Percussion devices- Tambourines and drums moreover have end up popular at some point of the Renaissance. They were commonly performed further to different gadgets.

Though the musical gadgets have been an crucial part of amusement, vocal music was more popular and generally heard than instrumental tune.

Dance

Dance turn out to be no longer as modern and freed from a movement as it is nowadays. There had been sorts of dances; u.S. Dances and courtroom dances. Country dances allowed anybody to participate, at the identical time as court docket docket docket dances had been handiest completed via professional dancers. Court dances additionally required formal clothing. Some of the maximum not unusual dance movements covered:

Reverence- This became a 'greeting' at the same time as dancing. Dancers face each one in every of a type as they slide their left foot back. Then, each knees are bent to bow to their associate.

Pavane- This was intended for gradual movements, so gowns and exceptional apparel is probably displayed. The pavane have become usually the first dance of the courts.

Saltarello- This upbeat dance required dancers to jump ahead 3 instances, then hop.

Italian Doppio- Also known as the Italian Double, this step required dancers to take lengthy, elegant steps ahead after which rise on their feet.

Ballet modified into created inside the direction of the Renaissance, too. It commenced out out within the courts of the nobles and subsequently spread to France. It come to be maximum famous even as Catherine De Medici dominated over the us of a.

Literature and Theatre

In the earlier days of the Renaissance, terrific men of wealthier households were generally educated. This constrained the spread of thoughts, as commonplace humans could not study them. However, literature have become greater digestible kinds of leisure, especially theatre. Putting on plays end up not unusual for entertainment, in particular later inside the Renaissance.

William Shakespeare

Even in recent times, Shakespeare is regarded as one of the fine writers of all-time. He is answerable for developing phrases which can be used within the English language nowadays (like bedazzled) and coined many idioms (like 'smash the ice'). Even his plot gadgets have been precise.

Shakespeare turn out to be born in 1564. Not an lousy lot is notion about Shakespeare's youth. After marrying at 18, he had 3 kids with a lady named Anne Hathaway. Several years later, they ended up in London. Here, Shakespeare worked with an performing enterprise organisation, Lord Chamberlain's Men.

Usually, there were approximately ten characters in a play. Young boys completed lady roles due to the truth ladies had been prohibited from acting at that point. Not only did Shakespeare act, but he moreover wrote performs for the group. Some of his maximum famous works protected A Midsummer's Night Dream, Romeo and Juliet, The Taming of the Shrew, and Richard III.

Lord Chamberlain's Men done on the theatre, however, they did not non-public the land. When the proprietor, Giles Allen, determined to tear down the theatre, the employer dismantled and relocated in the course of the Thames River. Eventually, the Globe Theatre can be constructed. This have become a massive playhouse, being able to preserve three,000 goal market people. Musicians made computer graphics noises, and a cannon fired blanks at important moments within the play.

Some of his later works covered Macbeth, Hamlet, King Lear, and Othello.

Other Notable Writers

While Shakespeare turn out to be one of the most famous Renaissance writers, severa others deserve a amazing point out for his or her contributions:

Geoffrey Chaucer- Chaucer wrote The Canterbury Tales, which have come to be a high supply of concept for Shakespeare. It changed into furthermore the number one intense piece of literature written in English, which emerge as considered a 'common' language on the time. Having it in English made it more to be had to the overall public.

Niccolo Machiavelli- Machiavelli's crucial paintings is his ebook, The Prince, which have grow to be purported to be a guidebook for rulers on a way to behave. However, a few historians argue it emerge as in reality a guidebook looking for to steer the loads to upward thrust up in competition to the authorities. Niccolo di Bernardo dei Machiavelli is credited as one of the maximum vital figures of political impact from the Renaissance. Machiavelli's e-book lay the inspiration for a way a political chief should behave. The Prince despatched the message a real chief is probably considered nearly holy with the aid of way of manner of the overall public, being a person that deserved to be accompanied. However, leaders must moreover be capable of commit evil on the equal time as it's far critical. This concept is one that could have a energy in the psychology situation as properly, as someone who's probably to do an evil act for non-public benefit is said to have a Machiavellian personality.

Dante Alighieri- The Divine Comedy is a poem that Dante wrote from his mindset of journeying through Hell. The poem has many religious issues and could be very complex, especially for the cutting-edge day reader. Despite its complexity, The Divine Comedy sticks out as one of the maximum stunning works in literature. Many people of the time disagreed with Dante's evaluations of Florentine politics, subculture, and society, however, the troubles can even be seen in present day-day day life-style.

## Chapter 4: Great Scientists and Discoveries during the Renaissance

With clinical discovery comes change. The give up of the Medieval Times is often referred to as the Dark Ages, as people had been not strolling towards gaining knowledge of extra about their existences. People have been a whole lot less hobby in arts and the sciences and extra hobby in faith. However, the Renaissance delivered approximately trade. Many top notch scientists of the time can be credited for the thoughts behind scientific exploration and the technologies which may be to be had to us nowadays.

Science within the Renaissance

There are many inventions in recent times which have been conceptualized or created for the duration of the Renaissance period. Even mind just like the clinical technique have been conceptualized and perfected, that's the idea of the way we take a look at theories and mind nowadays.

## Leonardo da Vinci's Scientific Contributions

While da Vinci is most referred to as being a awesome artist, he changed into taken into consideration an Italian polymath. Put certainly, this meant that he have become expert in lots of regions. Reports of da Vinci u . S . A . That further to being a excellent artist, he end up moreover an architect, musician, writer, inventor, mathematician, and scientist.

Da Vinci's drawings are a number of the maximum top notch from the time. Many discoveries sooner or later of the Renaissance should encourage later studies. Da Vinci pioneered the test of human anatomy and certainly one of a type clinical commentary. Da Vinci, being a 'Renaissance man' who excelled in masses of areas of human excellence, proved that artwork and the sciences might be mixed. For instance, endure in thoughts the manner online game characters circulate spherical in a faux international. The artful layout of the sector and the characters upload to gameplay and the enjoy, whilst the knowledge of physics and the human body is used to assist that individual skip via the arena in a extra attractive and practical way.

Even despite the fact that da Vinci may additionally best be appeared for his artwork, he is responsible for conceptualizing many extremely good mind, alongside side a calculator, the double-hull layout of a deliver, sun energy, an armored automobile, and a helicopter. However, the substances to be had in the route of da Vinci's lifetime by no means allow him deliver those thoughts to moderate.

Some of da Vinci's smaller upgrades had been applied in manufacturing on the time, together with a gadget that tested the tensile strength of wire and an automatic bobbin winder. Da Vinci is also stated for his contributions inside the fields of civil engineering, hydrodynamics, optics, and anatomy.

Francis Sir Francis Sir Francis Viscount St. Albans and the Scientific Method

Francis 1st Baron Francis Viscount St. Albans emerge as a specifically seemed philosopher. However, he is likewise credited for his artwork with the clinical technique. Unlike the typical doctrines of Plato and Aristotle, 1st 1st Baron Verulam emphasized the importance of experimentation and presenting evidence with theories. He believed that information should be gathered and analyzed to find a theory. Once a concept changed into decided on, scientists need to find out a way to check and take a look at that idea. Publisher 1st baron verulam operated beneath the philosophy that with the aid of organizing and looking at nature's truths, technological expertise may be used for the betterment of humanity. His mind have been rejected inside the beginning, specifically via Lord Burghley (Francis Francis Bacon's uncle) and Queen Elizabeth. However, after publishing the first e-book of Novum Organum Scientiarum in 1620, 1st Baron Verulam determined the honour of his buddies.

Sir Francis 1st Baron Verulam is concept for having said, 'expertise is power.' This perception is a few detail that has inspired many to attempting to find out an understanding of ideas via technological know-how. He helped create the divide among faith and philosophy by means of way of way of the usage of statement and deductive reasoning. Prior to 1st Sir Francis Bacon, humans had problem isolating the thoughts of philosophy from the ones of religion. Though every reputation on goodness to a sure volume, this separation emerge as crucial in dividing church and country as well. This separation went on to steer the political systems of nowadays as well, with the separation of the authorities from the church.

Francis Sir Francis Bacon's thoughts taught the importance of human idea. 1st 1st Baron Beaverbrook taught one-of-a-kind modes of inquiry and displayed the way to ask questions and are trying to find out a specific solution. Following the ones modes of inquiry is simplest natural, as humans have a curious nature. Without looking for an data of the vicinity spherical us, we considerably limit our capabilities and stifle ourselves in that area of innovative belief.

Other Inventions of the Renaissance

The Clock- The earliest clock become invented within the 1400s, after which, Galileo advanced it after inventing the pendulum in 1581. The invention of the pendulum extended the clock's accuracy.

Warfare- While the humans of the Middle Ages relied on castles for safety and knights for warfare, the Renaissance observed the invention of muskets and cannons, which labored the use of gunpowder and modified how conflict have become fought. Submarines have been moreover invented in some unspecified time in the future of this time.

Barometer- In 1643, Evangelista Torricelli created the number one running barometer. Inspired with the useful resource of Galileo, he observed how air pressure changed the extent of the water in a tumbler tube. The initial tube have become 35-ft tall—so early experiments have been accomplished on a grand scale. He tested tremendous liquids, locating that heavier liquids like mercury permit atmospheric strain be measured with a small tube.

Italic Typeface- Italic fashion writing end up invented in 1500 through manner of the usage of Aldus Manutius and Francesco Griffo. Manutius owned a printing organisation. The fashion have turn out to be first used on an illustrated call net page of a collection of letters with the useful resource of way of Catherine of Siena. Italics are used to create emphasis these days. Manutius' proper purpose have emerge as to preserve area in writing, which could reduce paper fees, and to mimic cursive writing, an paintings shape that changed into completely for the rich which, in turn, furnished suitable business enterprise for his employer with company.

Robotic Knight- This superb format is each other of da Vinci's. He might also moreover furthermore have designed and performed this 'robotic' at a celebration on the house of Ludovico Sforza, the Duke of Milan. Da Vinci's format involved rigging a in shape of armor with wheels, gears, and a pulley tool. By operating the pulley, the in form of armor may animate. In 2002, da Vinci's layout have become examined and placed to gain success.

Anemometer- In 1450, Leon Battista Albertia designed the anemometer, a device to diploma wind pace. The simple format measured the incline of a disk placed perpendicular to the wind. Leonardo da Vinci and Robert Hooke would possibly each take a turn improving this invention for a more accurate analyzing.

Scuba Diving Gear- Da Vinci designed this invention at the identical time as in Venice, as water surrounded the island town. The layout protected a bell-shaped tool and respiratory tubes that sat above water, a protecting face mask, a leather-primarily based-primarily based absolutely diving in form, and goggles. Though da Vinci did no longer do that out himself, it can have stimulated the advent of a achievement scuba gear within the Forties. Jacquie Cozens built and efficaciously tested in 2003.

Discoveries in Astronomy

The technological information of the moon, planets, stars, and celestial our bodies in outer space is called astronomy. As humans explored the area round them, they also regarded beyond the planet they lived on. Prior to the Renaissance, humans believed the Earth changed into the center of the arena. Greek scientists like Ptolemy and Aristotle had theorized this idea many years earlier than.

## Nicolaus Copernicus

Nicolaus Copernicus is credited as the first to expand a heliocentric idea of the universe which places the sun because the center of the universe. Even despite the fact that that is what we recognise to be real these days, maximum humans laughed at this idea in the direction of the Renaissance.

## Galileo Galilei

Hans Lippershey created the primary telescope in 1608. But on the time, the invention modified into greater of a idea than had any sensible use. The telescope is probably used to look throughout a long way distances, however it became vain for reading astronomy. Galileo modified the design and improved the high-quality of the image produced via the lens, which permit him take a look at the planets. Among his discoveries have been the moons of Jupiter, sunspots, the levels of Venus, and the crater-crammed surface of the moon. Galileo even theorized that the moon pondered the solar's mild in place of generating its personal, which we recognise to be actual nowadays.

As Galileo studied the motion of the sun and those planets he want to peer, he agreed with Copernicus' earlier idea that the sun have become the middle of the universe. He explained his paintings in a well-known paper. However, the Catholic Church disagreed along alongside along with his thoughts. As punishment for his 'loopy' theories, Galileo changed into placed underneath house arrest.

Tycho Brahe and Johannes Kepler

Brahe emerge as a few other prolonged-term astronomy fanatic who studied the planets and stars, taking unique measurements and evaluating their movements. Later in his life, he took on a German astronomer, Kepler, as an assistant. Together, their paintings proved Copernicus' heliocentric concept. Kepler additionally wrote three criminal hints of planetary movement and charted the motion of diverse planets, proving that they moved in an ellipse rather than a circle.

Paracelsus and Medicine

Swiss-neighborhood Theophrastus von Hohenheim, seemed surely as Paracelsus, modified right right into a scientist and botanist born close to the prevent of the 15th century. He challenged scientific practices of the time, noting that many remedies provided via manner of medical practitioners really made their patients worse. He is answerable for a number of the earlier studies on drugs and chemical substances that helped heal. Paracelsus became also one of the first to take a look at the human diet plan and surroundings as feasible belongings of infection. This concept grow to be a high stride in treatment.

Sir Isaac Newton

Newton have grow to be born within the path of the quit of the Renaissance, so it's miles hard to argue whether or no longer or not he's a real Renaissance scientist or now not. However, Newton changed into considerably prompted by using the art work of the Renaissance scientists who came earlier than him. In his research, he observed the paintings of Copernicus, Aristotle, Kepler, Galileo, and Descartes. At first, Newton became now not inquisitive about publishing his ideas. He did not start recording them till pal and astronomer,

Edmond Halley, entreated him to proportion them with the world. When Newton wrote the Philosophiae Naturalis Principia Mathematica in 1687, Halley paid to have it posted. In this ebook, Newton defined the regulation of gravity and the 3 laws of movement.

These first rate discoveries are nonetheless used these days. Some of his ideas and improvements encompass:

## Chapter 5: Important Figures of the Renaissance

Humanism took keep in 14th century Italy. Whereas the Dark Ages had lost consciousness of what it imagined to be human, the ideas of this movement promoted the concept of man because the center of his non-public universe. Humanism insisted that people encompass their private achievements, be it in the hassle of technological know-how, literature, education, or the classical arts.

The concept speedy unfolds Johannes Gutenberg invented the Gutenberg printing press in 1450. Following that, it has come to be common practice for fantastic thinkers and humanist authors, alongside facet Francesco Petrarch and Giovanni Boccaccio, to write down and print texts. The texts have been distributed at some stage in Europe, significantly contributing to Greek and Roman lifestyle and values.

The unfold of humanism end up a paradigm shift from the idea of a vengeful God. Though faith has become no longer overlooked certainly, humanism challenged the concept that guy modified into no longer well worth something. It assigned price to human contribution to society. Humanism is similar to the liberal arts of in recent times, encompassing those areas of human have a take a look at like tune, art, poetry, information, philosophy, and literature.

The revival of arts and humanism did no longer usually suggest religion became an awful lot less vital. In fact, religion remained a crucial part of the thoughts inside the lower back of philosophy. People although preferred to do topics which have been considered 'first rate.'

However, they had been seeking out a happier lifestyles.

Erasmus (Desiderius Erasmus)

Erasmus is considered the great student of the Northern Renaissance. His vital contribution blanketed the vital observe of the records of the past, specifically the Church Fathers and the New Testament. Erasmus also analyzed traditional writings. He criticized some strategies of the beyond and endorsed new humanist strategies, pioneering reforms inside the church.

Erasmus significantly valued education over faith. Like many different students, he doubted the idea of an immortal soul. He additionally accomplished a important feature in information human nature. Erasmus believed human nature can be molded, encouraging better attributes and discouraging humans who've been unsavory. He believed that via education, any type of change became viable.

One of his most well-known books is Praise of Folly. This e-book become rife with irony, due to the truth the student started out out wondering his non-public capacity to spark change round him. He maintained that, "Even the smart man want to play the fool if he desires to beget a little one."

Education During the Renaissance

Major shifts were taking area in educational systems. In the Middle Ages, novices were inquisitive about theology, properly judgment, and metaphysics. They desired to understand how the area worked. Humanists were superb in their gaining knowledge of goals. They sought training in colleges that emphasised records and literature, running to beautify questioning, writing, and talking. Pier

Paolo Vergerio (1370-1444) as quickly as said that the research of the time were liberal due to the fact they had been 'worth of a free guy.' Rather than a specific kind of learning, faculties emphasised the purpose of growing character and making ready university college college students for civic interest. Education mixed ancient research of the Greeks and Romans with extra modern-day-day-day teachings from medieval instances. The concept of doing what modified into relevant and working in the direction of morality moreover aligned with the Christian values of the time, without being as extremist because of the reality the Middle Ages.

Many of the adjustments in training have been added about via the present day mind of humanism and the manner it recommended human beings to count on for themselves. They had been not residing in step with a inflexible, unchangeable code however thinking the arena round them. Through inquiry, human beings started out to apprehend the arena. This thinking introduced on many medical, architectural, and tremendous tendencies.

Francesco Petrarca and Education

Francesco Petrarca, or Petrarch, is credited with the revival of classical getting to know. Known as a poet of his time, Petrarch became maximum of the primary Italian writers that strayed from medieval studying or scholasticism. Scholasticism had the motive of achieving an statistics or fact. Language grow to be no longer presupposed to inspire emotion or ask questions, but to offer fact. The problem come to be that scholasticism eclipsed what became called Augustinian tradition. Petrarch have a look at Saint Augustine's works and located out greater approximately the humanist branch of learning which targeted on analyzing oneself. By looking and running inward, a person may also want to assure his or her very own salvation. Through literature, track, and the humanities, people want to cultivate a totally unique courting with God. Traditional training centered on arithmetic, natural technology, properly judgment, and the study of divinity, but human beings taken into consideration the ones topics insignificant. While there was still a place in the sciences, one ought to moreover look at philosophy and its software program in the actual international. Only with the aid of way of becoming a hold near of idea might also need to at least one skip directly to a more vicinity in life.

Of direction, some of Petrarch's thoughts can be attributed to Dante's writing. Dante lived previous to the Renaissance, but humans accept as proper with he anticipated the upcoming revolt within the course of the Christian church. Dante died earlier than he noticed the revolution, however Petrarch helped set his thoughts in movement.

Rene Descartes

Rene Descartes, born in France in 1596, have grow to be a scientist, mathematician, and reality seeker, in addition to one of the first to wasteland traditional scholastic techniques added with the useful useful resource of Aristotle. Descartes moreover added thoughts-body dualism, that is the life of the mind and body as separate entities. This idea founded the concept for early psychology. Like Francis publisher 1st baron verulam, Descartes additionally insisted on technological records and evidence in desire to accepting theories as reality. He is responsible for the medical method of deductive reasoning, which he wrote about in his books Discourse on Method in 1637 and Rules for the Direction of the Mind in 1628 (even though the latter have become not published until 1701). Descartes' requirements can be separated into four thoughts:

Do not take transport of something as reality that you do no longer recognise as reality for yourself

Always divide issues into their only elements

Begin with clean and preserve to the complicated while problem-fixing

Always recheck reasoning

Like many astronomers earlier than him, Descartes believed the sector become no longer the center of the universe. However, the Catholic Church have become although suppressing this concept at the time, particularly in Rome. After writing his e-book on this, The World, Descartes discovered Galileo changed into suppressed and retracted his e-book.

Discourse on Method modified into moreover great as it changed into an essential philosophical artwork that became now not written in Latin. Instead, Descartes wrote in French, which become fantastic on the time. He believed this can make statistics available to genuinely all of us, such as women. Discourse moreover provided a ethical code that each one ought to observe when searching for the truth.

Another primary artwork by using manner of Descartes turn out to be Meditation on First Philosophy, in Which Is Proved the Existence of God and the Immortality of the Soul. This 1641 e-book included responses by using manner of philosophers of the time on numerous philosophical subjects, along with entries with the aid of way of Descartes himself. This feat modified into super at a time at the same time as differing thoughts and policies from rulers and the church suppressed versions in philosophical idea.

Other Influential Figures of the Renaissance

Of direction, at the same time as people with humanist ideas had a massive effect in this region, many others had a extremely good impact at the Renaissance period. Among people who deserve exceptional mentions are:

King Henry VIII- King Henry VIII became a man of many abilties. Like Leonardo da Vinci, he became regularly called a 'Renaissance man.' He may additionally need to talk 4 languages, had an appealing, confident appearance, was a musician and composer, an high-quality horseman, and a robust fighter. His crucial position became isolating the Roman Catholic Church from the Church of England, which in reality advocated the glide far from a vital religion.

Martin Luther- Martin Luther challenged the thoughts of the Catholic Church, in particular the concept that humans have to pay closely to get into Heaven. He additionally challenged the Pope's authority, mentioning that the Bible need to be the final word on whatever. His radical thoughts sparked a reform, bringing forth Protestant Christianity.

Catherine de Medici- As a more youthful female, Catherine have become captured to save you the Medici circle of relatives from attacking a metropolis-country. After convincing her captors that she desired to be a nun, she became allowed to live. Several years later, she married the King of

France and rose to energy as a queen. Later, her sons need to rule over Poland and France and her daughter might likely rule as Queen of Navarre.

Christopher Columbus- Though Columbus became not the number one to discover America, he did play a prime role in sparking new exploration via the Americas. Though he modified into attempting to find a shorter path to Asia or the East Indies from Spain, he got here upon the shoreline of America.

Vasco da Gama- This explorer completed a primary function in finding shorter trade routes. He traveled spherical Africa from Europe and arrived in India. This path was a good buy shorter than ones previously used, strengthening trade among the territories.

Joan of Arc- The Renaissance come to be a duration that carefully preferred male figures. Men were knowledgeable and ladies have been no longer. Typically, men had higher possibilities except for those girls who ruled as monarchs. Joan of Arc became a French military chief and made high-quality strides for women. However, she died greater younger after being burned at the stake at 19.

The Spirit of Humanism

Though individuals who examine humanism frequently take into account it an idea, humanism is actually a spirit of attaining human perfection via the expression of all of the ones matters people can try this animals cannot. It is the price of human existence. This concept, paired with increase inside the time and the exploration of recent thoughts, modified the future of humanity. It invited era, art work, and mastering on the identical time as doing away with the regulations of the church.

## Chapter 6: The Beleaguered Backdrop

From early Renaissance until mid-Renaissance (1400-1520 AD), the wealthy monarchies of Great Britain and France have been nevertheless stopping the Hundred Years War (1337-1453) with each unique.

Differences gravitated around land and people who controlled what land. The rulers in England were individuals of the House of Plantagenet and in France it turn out to be the House of Valois. Each u. S. A. Felt they'd right to the human beings, flora, objects, and the land that belonged to the alternative. What territories have been going to end up "vassal states" (subservient states) and which ones weren't, have come to be troubles of ultimate importance. It come to be an extended and bloody war of strength and can, but one that allow little input from the populations that labored the land, ran the generators, built the systems, and made the weapons for all of the armies to kill each different.

Realizing they were in reality pawns for the rich nobles and notables, peasants below the antiquated feudal device rebelled in England in 1381. Although the rebels lost, the spirit of upward thrust up wasn't vain. The Renaissance changed into a brand new age—a state-of-the-art dawn—and time for the vintage systems to disintegrate into facts. Every venture of those domain names craved upward mobility and freedom.

While England and France had been sorting out their lack of life social systems, Italy become already progressing steadily into the Renaissance—the period of rebirth. Their peninsula has become high-quality for commerce from new and long way flung lands. People from everywhere within the seemed worldwide were traversing Italy.

In their flowing gold-trimmed robes, people of every pores and pores and skin colour traded their wares of silver and gold, remarkable tapestries, spices to satisfaction every flavor, pigments crafted from foreign soils to pleasure every artists and commoners alike. Renaissance marketplaces have been like festive carnivals draped in silk and beads.

Under the oppressive feudal system that after prevailed, the buyers have been reviled. No longer have become that the case. The provider company training have been paramount, as they produced wonderful splendor and physical homes that towered over the heavy colorless stones of the darkish and dreary castles of vintage. The ancient splendor of Roman sculptures, literary writings, and philosophies of Greece resurrected. The rich nobles were clients of trade and the improvement of the highbrow and creative endeavors in their people.

Because of trade, there has been a thriving organisation of what would possibly these days be referred to as the "center elegance." They had the pricey of spending time conducting first-rate hobbies. Because the stoicism of the past become dwindling, people loved severa entertainments, whether or no longer or now not they be classical song or more banal delights.

This era grow to be characterised by means of using way of humanism. Humanism is a philosophy that specializes in the worthiness and virtues of the man or woman, no matter class or popularity. The human body became considered lovely in and of itself, no longer an event of evil for sexual perversion.

People were once more reading the Roman and Greek classics—the reminiscences of the gods and their graces, however for his or her symbolisms, not worship. Homer's Iliad and Odyssey, Virgil's Aeneid, Seneca's Medea, and Marcus Aurelius' Meditations all over again hit the limelight.

Then new Renaissance writers rose up like Erasmus (1466-1536) and Shakespeare (1564-1616). People had been encouraged to examine and write about the philosophical nature of man, metaphysics, the natural legal pointers, the power of human emotion, and the meaning of lifestyles. Poetry rose excessive as an art work shape. The humans placed out the vintage philosophies of Plato, Epicurus, and Aristotle. Religion though accomplished a dominant function however it modified into studied in a current moderate.

No longer did studying encompass blind repetitions of scripture, however getting to know became theology and there had been analyses of various translations and research of the scriptures in many cultures and traditions. Humanism propagated a proclivity for discussing and improving the quality in guy, in place of assuming he's an evil being in want of wonderful punishment and condemnation.

Objects of art, artwork, sculpture, and structure glorified now not most effective God however guy. It emerge as in a few unspecified time inside the future of the Renaissance that the stern traditions of Catholicism have been challenged through way of manner of others. During the 16th Century, Martin Luther tacked up his ninety-five theses on a church in Wittenberg, Germany. Following him, there were others—John Calvin, John Knox, William Tyndale, and Thomas

Cranmer. Unfortunately, faith has a bent to stimulate hostility, persecution, or perhaps warfare, that's what occurred in England, France, and Spain.

Medical understanding began to enlarge after the superstitious practices of the past were deserted. Once dissection changed into permitted thru the most vital Christian faith, the knowledge of illness and anatomy helped both physicians and artists.

Leonardo Da Vinci (1452-1519) rendered big drawings of the organs and bones of the human body, no longer most effective for the sake of the artists, but for budding physicians. Bloodletting, no matter the truth that though practiced in some factors, have become not the treatment of desire.

William Harvey (1578-1657) studied the circulatory system and that brought about recommended strategies of treating wonderful conditions. Herbs have been used as an beneficial beneficial useful resource for severa problems. Some had been marginally powerful. More records have become decided approximately bacteria and their position in the unfold of disease. Cleansing marketers which encompass wine have turn out to be pretty effective in killing bacteria.

Science in some unspecified time in the future of the Renaissance grow to be now not the dark vicinity of magicians and sorcerers. Enlightenment had come, and the astronomers studied the skies—not to assume the destiny, but to chart their way at the high-quality Mediterranean Sea and beyond.

Nicholas Copernicus (1473-1543) plotted the universe and proved that the movement of the earth and planets come to be heliocentric, that is, they revolved across the solar. Once the movie famous person positions had been well plotted, devices may be invented that aided in navigation both on land and at sea. The astronomers additionally found the manner to more because it ought to be plot the growing seasons.

Johannes Kepler (1571-1630) blended the legal hints of physics and astronomy and advanced a system for planetary movement that changed into a good deal extra accurate than individuals who had accomplished that earlier than.

Isaac Newton (1642-1727) produced the concept of gravity, the three felony pointers of motion, and moreover made a number of essential observations approximately the relationship of moderate and shade. Newton invented calculus.

Architecture at some degree within the Renaissance didn't really serve the reason of fortification from capability enemies. It come to be a party of the class of top, specially ornamental, and displayed home windows at the location. This society modified into open to the skies, to the earth, and the people who lived on it.

Bernini (1598-1680) is in all likelihood one of the most noted architects of the Renaissance, however there have been many others. He added a ultra-present day more active and flamboyant form to the sector of paintings—the Baroque. Like some of the opposite architects of the Renaissance, he no longer best designed buildings, however modified into city planner as nicely. His different pastimes had been sculpture in addition to painting.

Italy, mainly, grow to be a middle for mathematical enhancements. That become one of the first regions in Europe impacted with the aid of the Renaissance, as it come to be the center of trade. Monetary systems were crucial so investors may additionally need to conduct trade the use of the cash and currencies from many one of a kind global locations. Banking and finance grew there, as there have been goals for loans and with that a device of taxation. The Medici family emerge as the maximum vital and most a success banking entity of the time.

Art, sculpture, and portray flourished. Every constructing erected in a few unspecified time inside the future of the Renaissance showcased the art work of many artists and artisans. The art work accompanied the classical fashions, however there were some variations excellent function of the artists themselves. Michelangelo (1475-1564) sticks out as one in every of crucial bendy artists of the Renaissance, having sculpted, painted, and produced blueprints for architecture, collectively with complete houses, altars, and facades. Perhaps da Vinci come to be even greater flexible, as he emerge as moreover an inventor.

While Great Britain and France have been strangling themselves within the Hundred Years War, Italy turn out to be geographically isolated from it. The massive crags and peaks of the Alps discouraged interference from the political factions that vied for control of the European continent.

From the 9th Century onward, Italy come to be a conglomeration of town-states, every dominated by means of way of a king or a duke. Those rulers weren't empire-builders like Charlemagne or the German Holy Roman Empire. The metropolis-states were alliances of human beings, at the entire with not unusual commercial enterprise hobbies. The most critical of the city-states have been: the Republic of Genoa, the Duchy of Savoy, the Duchy of Modena, the Duchy of Milan, the Republic of Venice, the Republic of Florence, the Republic of Siena, the Kingdom of Naples, the Kingdom of Sicily, and the Papal States.

There's No Art in War

Politics, as history attests, by no means changes through exceptional function of the perennial battle of political factions. This was moreover real of the metropolis-states of Italy. There have been constantly struggles over electricity. Due to the upward thrust of the carrier provider class, loads of those conflicts have been mediated with the useful useful resource of the have an effect on of the issuer company commands. France placed an forestall to that.

In 1492, the Italian League, which have been underneath the robust manipulate of Lorenzo de Medici, collapsed on the same time as he died. Then the cultural and creative development of Italy have become slowed by way of using way of the incursion of Charles VIII of France in 1494.

Charles have become succeeded with the aid of Louis XII who captured the Duchy of Milan in 1500, after which he annexed the Kingdom of Naples in 1516. Louis come to be succeeded with the useful resource of Francis I (1494-1547).

Francis modified into now on pinnacle of things of Milan however preferred to deliver the exceptional wonders of the Renaissance to his neighborhood u . S . A . Of France. As a greater younger student, he were seeped in the humanism that characterized the Renaissance.

In the early sixteenth Century, the splendor of the Italian Renaissance hadn't quite reached France, and Francis bemoaned the reality that France didn't definitely have masses as a finely crafted sculpture to call its non-public. So, he imported the Renaissance to France by manner of luring in Leonardo da Vinci together along with his incredible Mona Lisa. In addition, Francis added in Rosso Florentino and Benvenuto Cellini promised to observe when his Italian assignment for Pope Clement VII was entire.

Francis I's efforts modified into interrupted by manner of the Holy Roman Emperor, Charles V, who craved control of all of Italy and its Papal States specifically. The Pope, Pope Clement VII, allied himself with Francis I, who end up already an avowed enemy of the emperor.

Clement modified into associated with the famous Medici family of Florence and the connection some of the popes and Italy have grow to be a sturdy one. The yr became now 1527, and loads of German, Spanish and even some Italian squaddies raced in. Unfortunately, Emperor Charles V received the warfare in opposition to the French. But that's now not the worst of what happened.

The Holy Roman Emperor lacked the price range to pay his squaddies! Needless to say, they were angry so they coerced their sub-commander, Duke Charles III of Bourbon to manual them to Rome. Once the mutinous squaddies reached Rome, they 1/2-destroyed the town and stole its treasured treasures and destroyed the facades of many homes, especially on Capitoline Hill within the coronary heart of Rome. This destruction persisted for a whole twelve months. This horrendous occasion have become referred to as the "Sack of Rome."

Michelangelo and designers needed to repair a number of the destruction this sacrilegious act triggered. Even in recent times, a few facades are despite the fact that missing.

Curiously, it have become Benvenuto Cellini—the sculptor whom King Francis had asked to introduce the Renaissance—who killed Duke Charles of Bourbon. Cellini end up a temperamental artist who despised seeing the capital town with all its art work grew to end up in to rubble, its statues stolen, and its glittering marble ripped off the houses of the noble metropolis of Rome.

To make subjects worse, the Pope needed to get away to his summer time house at the Castel Sant'Angelo. Then the imperial troops raced at some stage within the stone bridge and imprisoned him there.

After the troops withdrew, the wonderful Renaissance architect and sculptor, Michelangelo, and his group were despatched to Capitoline Hill to restore the harm. Their challenge became to update the broken facades and expand a few stone décor for the professional homes of important Rome.

Michelangelo come to be bowled over even as he observed what had come to be of the government homes of the first-rate town of Rome and its number one square. The as soon as-glowing region have grow to be plagued by using tents for the homeless; remains of rotting corpses despite the fact that littered the marble flooring; stains from dried blood had dulled the slabs that after composed the piazza, and stones from the senatorial constructing were scattered approximately.

The Renaissance placed its starting in Italy, however it regarded greater much like the stop, having been devastated through the usage of avarice and polluted with the aid of electricity. How did it thrive? This is the story of the humans and the locations that reawakened the outstanding, the actual, and the lovely.

It reignited wherein it started out out—with the individuals who made it show up, plenty of whom were in Rome and Florence.

## Chapter 7: The Medici Funding Of the Renaissance

Spread during the rolling hills and inexperienced spires alongside the tree-strains lay the cute splendor of the brown and inexperienced hills of Tuscany in Italy. Capped through carved square turrets stand majestic castles with surrounding cities with red-tiled roofs. It is a intense land for the sprawling banking organization of the Medici family.

Their overlords had been the fathers of fiduciary accounting, controlling almost all of the industries in their financial empire for over one-hundred years (1397-1499). The Medici Bank managed the fee range for the industries related to silk and cloth procurement and production, production, spinning and weaving, cleansing, mending, mining, timber finishing and dyeing. They engaged in global alternate and forex, bookkeeping, accounting, and ledger-keeping. The Medici's had monetary group branches inside the Papal States, Florence, Milan, Pisa, Rome, Venice, in addition to distant places places of work in Geneva, Avignon, Pisa, Bruges (Belgium), and London.

The Medici's furnished manipulate of the papal branch with a bribe. In trade for influencing church officials to hire Reverend Baldassare Cossa a cardinal, Cossa usurped Pope Gregory XII and feature become the "antipope," Pope John XXIII (no longer similar to the Pope John XXIII in present day years).

His throne have emerge as in Pisa, and there was every other pope in Avignon, France. Because of the non-public agreement some of the Medici own family and the Church prelates, the papal branches had been handled a hint in a different manner and included a fee for the top of the branches known as the "depositario generale."

The depositario generale modified into usually a prelate who modified into favored via manner of the use of the Medici's. Popes ought to order textiles and distinct wares—even collectively with artifacts and relics—at wholesale fees via a completely unique alternate organized for thru the Medici Bank. The Italian coin of the day end up the florin. Because it grow to be made of 24-karat gold, it's far equal to fifty-six cents in nowadays's American foreign exchange. Of direction, then as now, the price of gold fluctuates on the worldwide market.

Cosimo di Giovanni de Medici modified into the top of the Medici circle of relatives even because it rose into the attention of its power in the critical republic of Florence. The Republic of Florence come to be a republic in call only.

He managed and manipulated alternatives made through the elected municipal councils, or even those choices made through the "Signoria" or chiefs of the province.

One of the later popes, Pope Pius II, explained the actual underlying nature of this so-known as republic: Political questions are settled in Cosimo's residence. The man he chooses holds workplace. He it's far who makes a selection peace and battle. He is king in all however name.

Interfamilial rivalries with the aid of the anti-Medici celebration of the Strozzi and Albizzi families, alongside element the fiery noble, Palazzo Veccio, compelled Cosimo's exile in 1433. He settled for best a 12 months in Venice along along together with his son, Piero de Medici.

Cosimo have become a consumer of gaining knowledge of and the humanities, and that which fueled the Renaissance. While in Venice, he had an big library constructed for the people. Its architect became Michelozzo, who moreover designed many more systems for the town of Florence upon Cosimo's reinstatement in 1434. Cosimo executed his reinstatement and return to Florence via manipulation of the principle republican body, the Signoria, and a buy of favors from the noble households under them.

Cosimo changed into fairly adroit with putting in a balance of power inside the city-states of Italy, which supplied the usa with sufficient freedom to create majestic homes and outstanding works of art work.

It wasn't an easy feat due to the ongoing Lombardy Wars that raged to govern Venice and the Duchy of Milan in Northern Italy. The Lombardy Wars lasted on and off for thirty grueling years—1423-1454. The battle additionally spread to Naples and included Florence as nicely—each of which have been seats of the extraordinary treasures of sculpture, homes, and art work the location has even regarded. The Treaty of Lodi, signed in 1454, sealed that alliance for generations to go lower back.

Cosimo turn out to be moreover smart sufficient to encompass ecclesiastical officials in cordial affairs. He organized for the Pope at the time, Pope Eugene IV, to keep his church councils proper there in Florence, and invited the Eastern Holy Roman Emperor, John VIII, to go to and confer.

Cosimo and his own family preferred Florence decorated with the structure that could reflect simplicity and create pleasure. Cosimo hired the young Michelozzo, who apprenticed beneath the well-known Ghiberti and Donatello.

Michelozzo had the best functionality to combine the ancient styles that harked decrease back to antique Rome with the approaching Gothic styles of the day. The impact have become magical and interspersed with shade modestly positioned. Michelozzo designed the austere Palazzo Medici. Cosimo and his own family weren't modest. They preferred their likenesses reproduced for the edification of all. So, inner their palace, that they'd the painter, Benozzo Gozzoli, depict their likenesses as people of the Magi and their entourage.

Cosimo became one of the first men in records to open a public library. The e-book series consisted of manuscripts copied down the centuries by way of assiduous clergymen, similar to the Carolingian collection from the time of Charlemagne, works of Lucretius, Livy, Seneca, Plutarch, Cassio Dio, and plenty of others. In addition, Cosimo sent out creditors to exclusive components of the sector which includes Greece and Syria. The maximum noteworthy community humanist scholar, Nicolo de Niccoli, no longer first-class prepared the collection but contributed to it.

Cosimo set up the Platonic Academy. Cosimo's philosophy included that ascribed to with the useful resource of the humanists at the time. It changed into known as "Neoplatonism," due to its similarity to Plato's philosophy. There were not unusual elements most of the Neo-Platonists and the Christians, specifically their ideals in the divine principle of the "One." Thy believed in a awareness that would high-quality be translated due to the fact the "mind," "concept," "intelligence or the mind."

According to them, all fact in its manifestations depended upon the better ideas of "being" itself. Matter and the diversification of natural beings is an emanation of the handiest in phrases of a few aspect the senses can ascertain.

That it in reality is fabric has a starting and an prevent. Matter isn't immortal. The Neo-Platonists, for the most detail, supplied misleading postulates to provide an reason behind the connection many of the soul and nature. Philosophers like Marsillo Ficino faithfully adhere to the in easy phrases ontological rationales, this is, "If you could conceive of immortality, it need to exist."

Not all of the Neo-Platonists believed that the soul virtually is dwelling within the body, but the body gives it a physical manifestation by way of the usage of the use of which you can genuinely exist inside the worldwide.

Piero the "Gouty" succeeded Cosimo in 1464, but had a totally quick reign of 5 years. He grow to be called the "Gouty," due to the fact he did have gout, and became bedridden hundreds of his lifestyles. He officiated over Florence from his bedtable. He modified into despotic, as had been a number of the distinctive Medici's as nicely.

Florence have emerge as imagined to be a republic and public resentment towards the Medici's have emerge as fomenting. In addition, Piero's mind-set in the direction of the coping with of the loans within the Medici bank come to be so scrupulous and element-oriented that he called in loads of overdue loans. Compromise and negotiation might have been the better choice, but he become compulsive and tyrannical. Because so the various traders or even nobles have been going bankrupt, a tough and rapid planned a coup in 1466.

A former consultant of Piero's father, Diotisalvi Neroni, provided impetus to the coup and so did Borso d'Este, the Duchy of the city-nation of Modena. Piero's son and inheritor, the famous Lorenzo de Medici, surreptitiously investigated the rumors approximately this conspiracy and warned his father approximately it. Thus it have become thwarted and the lands and wealth of the perpetrators were confiscated.

During the subsequent yr, 1467, the Republic of Venice and the Duchy of Milan once more stirred up in rise up. One of the conspirators who had tried to degree a coup against Piero participated—Borso d'Este of Venice. He and a number of the nobles and illustrious, but disloyal families of Florence despised the reality that the Medici's have been genuinely ignoring the democratic nature of a republican shape of presidency and wanted to rid the Italian peninsula of the Medici's forever.

What's extra, the Duke of Milan additionally coveted an growth in their town-state. There were about thirteen thousand troops on every factor. The carnage occurred at the banks of the Idice River in Tuscany close to Northern Italy. This end up the number one battle in Italy in which firearms had been used, and led to seven-hundred bloody casualties collectively with one thousand horses, whose rotting corpses polluted the river waters for months to come.

That pollutants added approximately a loss of flowers and destruction of farmlands and plenty of sheep. Historians have determined that the outcome of the conflict modified into indecisive. It did bring about the Treaty of Lodi of 1454, which grow to be a pledge some of the warring city-states of Milan, Naples,

Florence, Genoa, and the Papal States to keep peace among them.

The nobles of the peninsula positioned out that extra threats to peace lay outside Italy, which encompass the hegemonic goals of the Ottoman Turks from the East. The nobles in preference to Piero the Gouty had been chargeable for the 40-three hundred and sixty five days duration of peace that followed and later have emerge as referred to as the Italic League. Piero turn out to be a sickly man who ultimately advanced lung illness in 1469 and died. His sons, Lorenzo and Giuliano then took over the Republic of Florence.

Banking in Italy then handed along to the 2 brothers. The human beings of Italy resented this common manage to be in the fingers of the tyrannical Medici's. Florence, in particular, which became the coronary coronary coronary heart of the Renaissance in Italy, become Medici-ruled.

Florence, even though, emerge as supposed to be a republic, wherein the human beings had a few balloting power.

Most of the cash the bank had manage of became generated with the useful resource of the complex banking hooked up order for the Papal States. The influential Pazzi own family wanted to wrest power far from the Medici's. They have been assisted through manner of manner of Pope Sixtus IV, his nephew, and Archbishop Salviati. Lorenzo and Guiliani were exceedingly famous some of the people because of the reality they regularly held banquets and carnivals for public entertainment competencies.

When the assassins tried to slaughter the Medici brothers, they were handiest able to kill Guiliani, but his brother escaped. The guards captured the Archbishop. Despite the reality that Salviati became a Roman Catholic prelate, he modified into hung from a window in one of the towers, and the crowd hatefully tore his body aside!

Lorenzo de Medici become known as "Lorenzo the Magnificent," as he became diagnosed for his benevolence. Above all of the Italian rulers, he changed into a purchaser of the humanities. During his reign, Michelangelo, Leonardo da Vinci, and Leon Alberti, as an author, rose to prominence and the sector in recent times is edified with the aid of the use of their paintings.

Lorenzo modified into succeeded thru "Piero the Unfortunate." He grow to be sincerely unlucky due to the truth he lived at the wrong time below unlucky times. The territorial jealousies interior Italy and the envies of the neighboring u . S . A . Of France delivered down the Medici's.

This had an full-size impact upon the proliferation of the arts and nearly halted the tremendous creative and literary accomplishments of the Renaissance. Even Michelangelo changed into forced to break out Rome.

In 1494, the older nemesis of the Medici's, the Sforza own family craved manage of Milan and despised the peace of the Italic League because it left him less powerful. He conspired with King Charles VIII of France, who additionally had an antique hereditary declare to Naples. He invaded Italy, and deposed the hapless Piero who drowned in the route of his haphazard escape. In his area, the invaders appointed a wild and fanatical priest by the selection of Girolama Savanarola. Artwork become smashed and burned inside the city squares by way of way of this scrupulous guy who made the people flip to a stoical adherence to faith.

The arts and literature of the Renaissance skilled a reprieve at some point of 1503-1521, beneath successive popes—Pope Julius II and Pope Leo X. Even the first-rate Michelangelo himself changed into referred to as once more to resume his exceptional work.

One of the maximum prophetic statements ever made in the history of the Renaissance become uttered with the aid of using Pope Leo X: "Now we are within the energy of a wolf, the maximum rapacious possibly that this global has ever visible. And if we do not flee, he's going to constantly devour us all."

**Chapter 8: Wolves of the Renaissance**

The motto of the Borgia circle of relatives have become: "Either a Caesar or Nothing."

While the Medici's had been the bankers of the Renaissance, the Borgia's were the energy-dealers. They have been of Spanish starting region, however—because of the truth some of the Borgia's have been popes, they've come to be entrenched in Italy at some level in the Renaissance.

After the lack of existence of the superb Lorenzo de Medici, Charles VIII of France invaded Italy to capture the Kingdom of Naples. His reign in Naples end up short-lived, however. Pope Alexander VI, one of the Borgia's, even though took over electricity via clearly controlling the College of Cardinals.

The pope have been married previous to his election and had kids thru that marriage. The popes in the ones days had on occasion been married and, similarly, had been stated to have had many love affairs with ladies and indicated that any youngsters born of those relationships were nieces and nephews. Alexander even had virtually considered one of his children, Cesare, made a cardinal. Cesare become legitimately born to him previous to his papal election.

To shield himself and Italy from the have an impact on of Charles VIII of France, who although desired to restore dominion over Naples, Pope Alexander VI joined in an alliance with Venice, the Duke of Milan, Ludovico il Moro, and King Ferdinand of Spain.

In 1497, tragedy struck. The bloated frame of the loved Duke of the tiny province of Benevenuto in Northern Italy changed into observed floating in the Tiber River. After that murder, the Pope done a active search for the culprits, and there has been sketchy proof that some of the servants had committed the homicide.

In the three hundred and sixty five days 1502, taken into consideration taken into consideration one among his cardinals, Cardinal Orsini, asked the pope for permission to visit the King of France who befell to be in Milan at the time. Orsini were a legate to France, so it would have seemed to be a logical request. Nevertheless, the pope refused. Regardless of the pope's prohibition, Orsini went besides.

Upon his pass decrease lower back, the pope had Cardinal Orsini thrown in to his dungeon, wherein he died twelve days later.

Alexander VI may have finished that due to the fact he heard the Orsini own family become conspiring to slay his son, Cesare.

The Orsini's and the Borgia's had been arch-warring parties. Chicanery and criminal behavior permeated the Roman Curia, head of the Roman Catholic hierarchy. It end up scandalous and the people of Church had been horrified to appearance such evil creep into the Church.

When Pope Alexander VI changed into growing older, his son, Cardinal Cesare, murdered his older brother, Giovanni, if the rumors are to be believed. That supposed if Cesare changed into to give up from the priesthood and cardinalate, he should inherit his father's wealth.

Cesare additionally desired the principality of all of Central Italy, so he stimulated the papal enclave so that they might pick out Giuliano della Rovere as the following pope. Cesare and della Rovere had an settlement: if Rovere have end up the following pope, Cesare must keep all his honors and titles. Rovere, but, betrayed Cesare and they have become fierce enemies. Cesare have become ruthless, and it's miles stated he turn out to be responsible for different murders.

Back in 1494, Pope Alexander VI preferred manipulate of Naples, so he prepared for Cesare to marry Carlotta of Naples. When Carlotta refused, King Frederick IV of Naples secretly had Alexander's daughter, Lucrezia Borgia, marry Alfonso of Aragon.

In July of 1500, hired assassins tried to kill Alfonso due to family rivalries among the Orsini's and the neighboring Colonna families. When Alfonso didn't die, even after a month had surpassed, armed men entered his bedchamber and strangled him to dying.

Rumors persist within the information books to at the moment that Cesare became responsible, and probably even

Pope Alexander VI himself had the dastardly deed done.

Lucrezia Borgia, the daughter of the pope, were married earlier than to Giovanni Sforza, a super Count and Lord. That marriage have been prepared with the useful resource of manner of the pope himself. As it grew to grow to be out, the Sforza own family changed into of no extra help to the pope politically. When the pope now not want to see any advantage for that union, he planned on getting rid of him. Lucrezia' brother, Cesare, warned her and Giovanni fled. Later on, the pope annulled their marriage.

In 1502, Lucrezia married Alfonso d'Este, the Duke of Ferrara. Pope Alexander VI organized that marriage. Lucrezia emerge as extraordinarily cute and supplied the visage of a reputable and extremely good Renaissance female. However, she wasn't. She had an extended a torrid love affair collectively at the side of her private brother-in-regulation, Francesco II Gonzaga of Mantua. Most in all likelihood, Francesco wasn't her nice lover, as he reduced in size syphilis and they had to break off the affair.

Lucrezia then had a passionate love courting with the poet, Piertro Bembo. It is stated they exchanged a number of the most transferring love letters ever written.

Gioffre Borgia (1482-1516) come to be Pope Alexander VI's youngest son. He became married to Sancha of Aragon, and that gave him the familial connection to the Kingdom of Naples because of the truth she became the daughter of Alfonso II of Naples. He turned into just twelve at the time he married. The Pope married him off in exchange for Naples recognizing the sovereignty of Alfonso's declare to the throne at Naples.

The pope's manage of Naples lasted till 1494 while the King of France, Charles VIII (see Chapter One) invaded Italy, as a result starting the Italian Wars. When that befell, the cowardly Alfonso II fled Naples. Gioffre's companion, Sancha, had severa incestuous love affairs with Gioffre's older brothers, inclusive of the infamous Cesare.

In 1499, Charles successor, Louis XII, wasn't content fabric with Naples, however seized Milan, and exceeded along Naples to Spain. Pope Julius II turn out to be then pope. This pope changed into moreover referred to as the "Warrior Pope," as he made an alliance with Maximillian I of Spain and unique the League of Cambrai in 1508. The allies then drove Louis XII out of Milan and Italy.

Michelangelo designed an altar façade for Julius II, which included the arena-well-known sculpture, Moses, finished in 1515. A short-lived peace emerge as secured beneath Francis I of France, who changed into furthermore a consumer of the arts. As end result of wars, Francis changed into unable you got any bounty from Italy and come to be coerced into signing the Treaty of Madrid in 1526.

This alliance thwarted Cesare's plans because of the fact the French had been now in Milan. With his father no longer in electricity, Cesare had no have an effect on over the papal curia. He himself have emerge as gravely unwell and left Rome. He had supported Cardinal della Rovere for the following pope, however della Rovere pulled out his guide from him, and had to surrender a number of his lands and titles. Cesare changed into arrested for all his meddling into Papal affairs, and on the identical time as released—have end up arrested all over again thru Ferdinand of Aragon. After that confinement, Cesare died in a minor skirmish.

Lucrezia become the best Borgia who changed into although lively. She became in the long run freed up for all of the political entanglements and organized the kingdom with sophistication and charm. Under her patronage, arts and song flourished over again.

### Chapter 9: Art Leonardo Da Vinci

In 1480, Leonardo modified into an achieved artwork apprentice beneath Verrochio at genuinely one of most prestigious workshops in Florence.

Not first-class have grow to be he a painter, however he sculpted as well. In time, he have become called an inventor. De Vinci came below the have an impact on of the Medici circle of relatives and studied on the Neo-Platonic Academy.

His first price covered a portray for the Hall of the Five Hundred, inside the Palazzo Vecchio. This changed into a strong, multi-tale constructing intended to be the Town Hall for Florence. It had three courtyards, a second ground whole of impressively-named suites and houses for dignitaries.

It turn out to be in that Hall that Leonardo worked with Michelangelo, his imaginitive cutting-edge-day. On the wall Leonardo grow to be assigned, he have become to render a portray of the Battle of Anghiari, an outline of a warfare among Milan and the Italic League in opposition to Florence in 1440.

This has been called the Lost Painting of da Vinci, due to a misjudgment on his aspect. It changed into painted as a "Buon fresco," that may be a painting rendered on wet plaster—or intonaco. As the plaster is drying, the pigments integrate with it and the portray then hardens. There are different styles of frescoes: 1) secco painting, which combines the pigments with a binding liquid—on the aspect of egg tempera, oil, or glue; and multiple) paint done immediately to a semi-wet intonaco floor.

He used a kind of plaster now not typically used, however his trying out of it had validated a achievement. On the day he labored at the painting, the climate turn out to be wet and damp. Artists usually draw the snap shots first on a huge paper in graphite or charcoal and switch it at once to the floor of the plaster. That is called a "caricature" and is used as a manual for doing the fresco itself.

Some of these cartoons are so well-finished they have been displayed as quantities of art work themselves. Unfortunately, Leonardo's caricature slid off the ground of the wall plaster because of the advanced humidity of the day and ended up at the ground! The relaxation of it needed to be deserted at the same time as colorings he turn out to be using ran down the wall.

The architect, Giorgio Vasari, then had the wall covered over with a contemporary wall. Art scholars and professionals have attempted to find out the piece thinking about the fact that then, but with little success.

The Augustinian clergymen commissioned him to colour Christ as an little one with Mary the Virgin, at the side of the adoring Magi for his or her chapel. He had heard that Lodovico, who've become the regent in the Duchy of Milan, modified into looking for navy engineers, architects, sculptors, and painters.

Artists needed to make a great residing and desperately had to locate benefactors who also can need to offer quite some paintings for them at excessive charges. The life of an artist and an inventor movements from task to hobby, and the excellent way to ensure long-term artwork is to discover human beings who have the sources to pay for it.

Leonardo, whilst he doodled, designed all styles of implements and had a know-how of advent from having completed limitless designs for homes. Anxious to go away the confines of a monastic chapel in Florence, Leonardo wrote a lengthy letter to Lodovico approximately his many skills.

It take a look at like a 3-web page resume, and inspired Lodovico. Of course, Leonardo had higher credentials as a painter, so Lodovico requested him and his colleague Giovanni Ambrogio to color Virgin of the Rocks for the Chapel of the Immaculate Conception. The chapel come to be built through Lodovico's accomplice for the Church of St. Francesco Grande in Milan. It modified into to be paid for via the Confraternity who ran the Church. There modified proper right into a dispute over making the closing charge in 1483, as agreed to in the settlement.

The Confraternity could in all likelihood simplest make a lesser price on it, so Leonardo and Giovanni asked Lodovico to intervene. Instead of insisting the total rate be made, he suggested that specialists study the piece. After further appeals, the 2 artists weren't able to get the overall fee. In the interest of peace, they settled for masses less.

By manner of military engineering, da Vinci created a revolving bridge for Duke Sforza. In order to reveal the bridge, da Vinci established a rope-and-pulley tool set on wheels. There became a counterweight on the other end for stability. This became used for the fast transit of infantrymen for the duration of warfare. For marvel attacks, Leonardo advanced a scuba-sort of outfit. It changed into composed of a leather-based totally-based totally suit ready with a bag sort of masks for the diver's head. From that, a cane have become extended vertically so the diver need to breathe, and there was a cork related to hold it floating at the floor.

To it, a balloon turn out to be attached so the diver ought to inflate or deflate it, relying upon whether or now not or now not he favored to ground or no longer.

He changed into then commissioned to color the Last Supper, his maximum famous portray. It become done for the Church of Holy Mary of Grace, an critical church for Lodovico and his family. Lodovico's wife have become interred at that church in 1497. The Last Supper wasn't relocated to a national gallery; it's miles though there and displayed inside the refectory of the Dominican nuns in their convent adjacent the Church.

It wasn't completed as a buon fresco; it modified into painted in oil and tempera on dry plaster. To beautify the highlights of the figures, he sealed the image in a skinny coat of white plaster to which he implemented a coating of white lead to the oil layer. White lead is a white color with undertones of crimson to make the faces seem warm. As the lead in it's miles toxic, it's miles quality blended at the ground above the tempera for protection competencies.

In 1482, the Duke of Milan commissioned Leonardo to create a huge bronze horse in his honor. Da Vinci come to be acquainted with bronzing, as he used it to expand canons. This horse emerge as designed to stand at the height of twenty-four ft. The machine with bronze is to create a clay, life-duration model for the mold, melt the bronze and unfold it over the decide. This took him years to do with the primitive device of the fifteenth Century.

The statue required eighty hundreds of the bronze. As he became making equipped the bronze, but, the pope and King Charles VIII interrupted his work. Pope Alexander VI desired to rid Milan of Lodovico Sforza, so bloody skirmishes broke out in Milan. (see Chapter Two) Leonardo and his assistants then fled Milan.

In order to prevent King Charles access into Milan, the duke bribed him with the unused bronze Da Vinci had deliberate upon for the statue. He then had the bronze melted down over again and converted in to canons. After the wars have been quelled, the infamous Borgias assumed manage of Milan. Once the Borgia's had been set up, Leonardo end up commissioned in 1502 through the infamous Cesare Borgia, one of the sons of the pope.

This time, Leonardo's exceptional skills were hired. He labored as a navy engineer designing the fortified town of Imola and mainly drawing focused maps of Italy. Experts have said that his maps were relatively correct and centered. After that challenge grow to be whole, Leonardo toured spherical Italy supplying his developers with plans for strongholds inside the path of the location.

One of the favourite situation subjects for the Renaissance artists and designers changed into the try to format flying machines. Leonardo Da Vinci emerge as extremely good for his many innovative designs. Bats and birds had been the favored models for Da Vinci's sample. He referred to as it an "omnithopter." The latter time period fine defined his sample for a tool he deliberate that sincerely resembled in recent times's helicopter.

In 1488, he sketched some different device that became designed to preserve a person, who have become to fly in a inclined position in this stomach. There were controls for turning the 2 fingers of the form. Another format he rendered resembled the wings of a bat which the pilot need to control with an up-and-down motion, much like that of a bat.

He moreover designed an armored automobile. It become a turreted form strengthened with metal plates and hooked up on wheels underneath. Guns were to be located in a round sample that allowed for turning. It took 8 men to function the device.

As every different weapon for war, Da Vinci designed a large crossbow. It measured about twenty-seven yards in the course of, and the "arrows" were clearly rocks. Cranks were used to fireplace them.

The soldiers inside the 15th Century used cannons, of direction, however they have been desk positive. Leonardo advised using a cellular canon. It became a triple-canon that might be loaded from the the front, as conventional. It modified into designed like others that he had drawn (and used) like mobile ladders.

Although he didn't invent the clock, Leonardo made it more correct. In the fifteenth Century, they really had pendulum-operated clocks. Da Vinci invented this clock in area of genuinely draw it out. The clock had mechanisms—one for minutes and the alternative for hours. Instead of the usage of pendulums for every operation, he used springs—an creative concept.

In addition to his unique innovations, Da Vinci used springs to propel a cart. When the prevent was launched, the wheels could in all likelihood flip and the car may additionally want to "spring" in advance. He included that idea in to growing a robot man. Mostly the "guy" moved thru pulleys related to springs. It had to be guided, but must stand, take a seat, and bend over.

As referred to in Chapter One, King Francis I of France hired Da Vinci to go lower back to France and inaugurate the Renaissance there. Da Vinci changed into aged with the resource of then. During his closing years, he worked on a mechanical lion that King Francis I desired. It became designed to walk beforehand and its chest may be opened to show a stone bouquet of lilies. He additionally reportedly designed a grand round stone staircase at the Chateau Rochefoucauld.

The Chateau, first built within the eleventh Century, is in Southwestern France and continues to be inhabited through descendants of a Duke and Duchess. Most of the massive stone turreted citadel is used as a museum in which lots of Da Vinci's works are displayed.

Da Vinci died in 1519, lamenting the fact he hadn't dedicated sufficient time to his artwork.

## Chapter 10: Michelangelo

Like Leonardo da Vinci and a number of the opposite Renaissance artists, Michelangelo (1475-1564) had his begin in Florence.

Florence end up a republic, and most of the strength have end up exercised by means of using way of the nobles who have been a part of the "Signori," or city council.

In time, the ruling families of Italy—the Medici's and the Borgia's—have become extra tyrannical. All the architects, sculptors, artists, and writers of the Renaissance in Italy were interrupted through manner of the use of wars, insurrections, and the fluctuation of the political scene.

Michelangelo apprenticed at the workshop of Domenico Ghirlandalo, whose essential knowledge changed into fresco portray. Ghirlandalo and his college students completed the partitions of the Sistine Chapel. Michelangelo is famous for his later art work on the ceiling and behind the altar in that structure. The younger artist modified into pleasant fourteen even as he commenced out, and that have become uncommon. Michelangelo towered above his fellow university college students in ability, challenge, and knowledge. For that cause, Michelangelo's father turn out to be in a role to persuade Ghirlandalo to pay him wages in location of really pay for his preserve, which became the commonplace exercising.

The participants of the Medici family had been fervent customers of the arts. Michelangelo changed into accompanied as a member of his court docket docket a good way to create the ones works of paintings. As bankers, the Medici's knew the price of art work, as well as its rate for influencing particular dignitaries in Europe.

In 1492, Michelangelo become commissioned through Lorenzo de Medici to sculpt a treatment for him. The become aware of changed into Battle of the Centaurs, a instance of a classical war. Renaissance artists frequently used troubles from records and the classics as fashions for his or her paintings. The marble relief is sensible, however shows the exaggerated musculature that turned into very everyday of the Renaissance. That fashion is known as "Mannerism."

Lorenzo de Medici died in 1492. Once that passed off, Michelangelo knew the most constant location for him changed into back domestic. He grew up in Tuscany and stayed together with his father and deliberate on staying till Florence became lower again to a nation of normalcy. While at domestic, he acquired a large block of marble from Northern Tuscany to carve a big statue of Hercules. There were quarries mined for the stunning Carrera marble. This marble end up surprisingly veined in blue-gray and particularly famous most of the Renaissance sculptors for its sturdiness and texture. It changed into difficult, yet gentle sufficient to carve rounded shapes with out chipping. Carrera marble had been used for the cause that time of Ancient Rome.

There is a dispute among students as to whether Michelangelo did the piece to promote later for Lorenzo de Medici. The 8 foot high statue were lost to time at the same time as Piero emerge as deposed due to the interference of the wild and loopy monk, Girolamo Savonarola. That monk preached a pass lower back to a greater stoic manner of lifestyles, and have end up horrified thru depictions of nude figures and the carving of figures for self-aggrandizement, due to the reality the Medici's and rulers were wont to do. Savonarola made it a weekly workout to gather up treasured works of artwork, take a mallet and ruin them. Then he may additionally want to burn them inside the city rectangular as defined earlier.

Artists had been searching for paintings within the ones days and in 1494, after doing some reconstructive artwork on a chapel in Bologna, the Shrine of St. Dominic. Desperate for money, Michelangelo then rendered a small piece known as Sleeping Cupid, and handled it with acid so it might appear to be an historical artifact. He offered the Cupid to an art work dealer, Baldassare del Milanese. A cardinal, Raffaele Sansoni Riari, came at some stage in the piece and bought it. When he located it grow to be a fraud, he didn't charge Michelangelo.

Instead, he hired him to do greater paintings for him in Rome.

Upon seeing Michelangelo's artwork, Cardinal Jean de Bilheres-Lagraulas commissioned him to carve the well-known Pieta. Michelangelo carved this piece with first-rate reverence, and even used some "revolutionary license" to adjust the scale of the Christ figure as a way to healthy the frame of a entire-grown guy into Mary's lap. His cutting-edge biographer, Giorgio Vasari, said of it, "The candy air of the top and the harmonious turning into a member of of the arms and legs to the torso, with the pulses and veins, are mind-blowing."

Michelangelo's pals requested him to head returned to Florence, as a chunk of marble he had saved in his studio had been partially destroyed at the same time as an inferior sculptor attempted to artwork the piece. Out of the very last marble,

Michelangelo carved his remarkable sculpture called David.

The political scenario in Florence have come to be in brief quieted and the republic modified into now being run with the aid of Piero Soderini. He modified proper right into a moderate and clever ruler, even though he lacked the strength to control the province from outdoor intruders. It modified into for the duration of that thing that Leonardo da Vinci, a rival, grow to be commissioned to color the Battle of Anghiara depicting a struggle among Milan and Florence waged in 1440.

Leonardo's fashion confirmed a first-rate deal of dynamic motion in his renderings, and emerge as more real to the context of the subject than Michelangelo. Piero Soderini commissioned Michelangelo to color the Battle of Cascina displaying a battle amongst Florence and the province of Pisa. Instead of a warfare scene,

Michelangelo planned on telling the story of the struggle which have come to be a marvel assault. He showed the Florentine squaddies bathing in a river within the approach of responding to a name to action by using way of their commander. Michelangelo have turn out to be very eager on showing nude male figures, so the tub scene allowed him to do that. It additionally accredited him to depict certainly one of his favored poses called the "contrapposto."

The contrapposto is a instance of the human determine displaying almost all of the weight on one leg whilst the rest of the frame is twisted in a position that showed he have emerge as equipped for pending movement.

Michelangelo in no manner completed that piece because of the fact he have become called to Rome with the aid of Pope Julius II. Julius II have turn out to be the "warrior pope," who regained manipulate of his Papal States from a rebellious corporation of nobles and the Borgia own family in 1516.

He emerge as moreover the Roman Catholic prelate who created the Swiss Guard to guard himself and all destiny popes from invaders. Julius emerge as rather self-focused and employed Michelangelo to sculpt an difficult tomb for himself. Knowing the pope's predilection, Michelangelo sketched out a tomb façade with twenty figures! The most important parent on this tomb changed into Moses.

It is likely the maximum charming decide ever sculpted via Michelangelo. It suggests Moses as he truly descended from Mount Sinai after receiving the Ten Commandments from God. The appearance of anger in his eyes comes from the biblical tale about how he observed the Israelis had original an idol, which was forbidden with the useful resource of their law. It is a effective manly determine that also suggests the idea of contrapposto, indicating he is set geared up to spring into movement. The "horns" on his head were without a doubt from a mistranslation from the genuine scripture that meant "rays," which means that there have been rays emanating from the pinnacle of Moses.

In 1508, Pope Julius II requested that Michelangelo pause in his artwork on Julius' tomb to colour the twelve apostles on the ceiling of the Sistine Chapel. Michelangelo turned into often challenged by way of the use of way of of his combatants, Raphael, the noted Renaissance painter, and Bramante, who have become an architect.

The guys knew that Michelangelo changed into lots more familiar with sculpting than portray, so they'll deliver that to his interest on occasion. He proved to the 2 of them that he, definitely, grow to be outstanding in painting as well. Although Pope Julius truely desired artwork of the twelve apostles, Michelangelo glad him to permit him more freedom of expression.

The ceiling has problems from the Old Testament, or even a few figures have been taken from mythology. Michelangelo, in comparison to Leonardo da Vinci, spent little region doing landscapes, so the ceiling is replete with human figures. It is concept that he painted the ceiling lying on his lower decrease back, because he complained approximately lower once more ache. He didn't do the ceiling mendacity on his once more, however. To do the ceiling, Michelangelo designed an intricate scaffold which he moved throughout the chapel as he advanced. The lower again ache advanced as it have end up usually critical for him to arch his yet again so that you can paint.

Michelangelo used the higher fresco method of portray on wet plaster. He might also need to first-class art work on small sections at a time because of the truth the plaster dried short. After it dried, Michelangelo included it with a really skinny layer of moist plaster. His use of coloration become one-of-a-kind from that of Da Vinci. Michelangelo used sharp and unexpected contrasts of colours even as Da Vinci labored with a gradual trade of colour to expose shading.

The Sistine ceiling depicts scenes from the Book of Genesis up till the tale of Noah and the Flood. Over 3 hundred biblical characters are painted on the ceiling.

In the 12 months 1520, the Medici own family who nonetheless lived in Florence, shrunk Michelangelo to carry out a touch art work on their circle of relatives's tomb and chapel. He carved what became referred to as the Medici Madonna for the heading of the façade. To one aspect is an enforcing statue representing night time time and day and to the opposite component: Dusk and Dawn. Lorenzo the Magnificent, Michelangelo's former consumer have become buried there on the aspect of 3 different people of the Medici family.

Michelangelo have become commissioned to format factors of the Laurentian Library for the Medici's. The Medici's have been—another time—expelled and Michelangelo fled to Rome.

In 1536, Michelangelo changed into commissioned with the aid of Pope Clement VII, who have become one of the

Medici's himself, to paint the Last Judgement at the again wall of the altar within the Sistine Chapel. After Pope Clement died, his successor, Pope Paul III cherished his paintings and insisted he give up it.

The Last Judgement turned into one in every of his most expensive accomplishments. As Michelangelo modified into now older, he wasn't disenchanted thru the complaint he now and again obtained via manner of his traffic, who knew little about the form of paintings that went into developing a fresco.

One precise person, Bagio Martinelli, vociferously criticized him because of the nudes. As a private comic tale, he rendered a likeness of Martinelli as a soul being led proper down to hell. Once Martinelli discovered the decide, he changed into incensed and complained bitterly to the Pope, insisting Michelangelo remove it. Pope Paul, who have been likewise aggravated with the useful resource of manner of the complainer, Martinelli, smiled and spoke back pronouncing there has been no longer some thing he ought to do approximately it... "Hell is not in my jurisdiction."

In the three hundred and sixty five days 1546, Michelangelo have become commissioned to remodel St. Peter's Basilica and Capitoline Hill. Since the Sack of Rome in 1520, the area grow to be in horrible circumstance. Not looking to be embarrassed by using using the usage of an upcoming visit with the useful resource of using Emperor Charles V, Pope Paul II hired Michelangelo to restore the layout in the marble ground of the out of doors square and do greater art work on the dome in some time. Because he have emerge as now in his seventies,

Michelangelo hired many architects and developers to carry out his designs.

Many of the marble slabs from the rectangular were robbed at some level in the Sack of Rome, so Michelangelo cleverly redesigned it as a trapezoid. He then took an historical statue of Marcus Aurelius and located it inside the middle of the square in the front of the govt buildings on Capitoline Hill.

Michelangelo became a very pious guy and lots of his works have been like prayers in movement. He frequently pondered the deep non secular which means of each piece. On one event, he wrote: "Lo! You are precise... Pity my state of evil, cleanse and hide it—So close to to dying am I, up to now from God, forlorn."

Michelangelo died within the 12 months 1564 at the age of eighty-8. He was buried in his liked Florence.

## Chapter 11: Hans Holbein

Once King Francis I had carried the art of the Renaissance to France, phrase approximately its beauty unfolds.

Leonardo Da Vinci have emerge as there and his reputation grew an extended way and huge. While Leonardo and Michelangelo created works of beauty in Italy, the taste of the Renaissance reached the Holy Roman Empire of Germany.

A more youthful guy via the selection of Hans Holbein (1497-1543) grew up in an innovative own family, as his father, too, have end up a painter. Following the Italian artists and architects, the artisans of Germany began out making metallic molds and woodcuts for printers. The Guttenberg Press of the past due fifteenth Century modified into being advanced for additonal imaginative portions similarly to for type. Humanism had its affect as properly, and figures weren't merely biblical; they have been pics of notables. The margins and empty regions of e-book pages had been embellished with sketches in ink and sepia.

Holbein's woodcut designs for his introduction the Dance of Death, and what became known as "Icones," of representations of Biblical problems for the bible saved through a circle of relatives and passed on from generation to generation. Most of the Bibles had been the conventional Latin Bible, but a contemporary bible had been observed—now in vernacular English—the Tyndale Bible inside the early 16th Century. This coincided with the Protestant Reformation while there has been a split amongst strict adherence to the Roman Catholic time table.

Holbein's paintings in print format coincided collectively together with his innovative fashion on the identical time as he become commemorated with being commissioned to layout the cover for Martin Luther's Bible—the bible created for the Lutheran faith within the early sixteenth Century. The have an effect on of humanism entered into philosophical idea, and the human body end up taken into consideration adorable and correct. Religion became not a thriller written extremely good in Latin for the Royalty.

Furthermore, religion modified into no longer taken into consideration the most effective appropriate issue for Renaissance paintings. Hans Holbein painted paintings of art for the Council Chamber and the corridor of Dance in Basel, Germany. Renaissance dance emerge as the style of dance inside the royal courts. It later spread to the countryside as well.

Influence of the Humanism of Eramus

Until the later fifteenth Century there was a shift internal spiritual thinking that become more utilitarian. It sought to interpret spiritual truths now not as Biblical representations, however as thoughts associated with morals and ethics. It wasn't atheistic—pretty the opposite—but placed duty upon the individual for interpreting and dwelling everyday with the Christian thoughts. It shied far from excessive pageantry however became Christianity in workout.

Philosophers of this school of concept had been referred to as humanists. They had been devoted to their proclaimed religions, but at a loss for words amazing doctrines and practices inside their respective faiths. Humanism coincided with the Protestant Reformation, while Christian religions other than Roman Catholicism arose. It required crucial assessment of abuses that got here up in the Roman Catholic religion, basically being enacted with the aid of the clergy. Its purpose end up reform.

Perhaps the nice version of Christian humanism for the duration of the Renaissance became Erasmus. (see Chapter Eight) He became a Catholic priest who remained real to Catholicism, but have emerge as essential of the abuses that had crept in to the Church, such as the loose set of morals that permit a celibate clergyman to have kids and recognition upon wealth in desire to the ethical steering of the honest. Erasmus emerge as a believer in unfastened will, a lifestyles of piety, and fashion.

Erasmus rejected the seriousness of faith, implying there was pleasure in its exercise. There turn out to be additionally a freedom that comes from satisfaction. He believed that Christians are entitled to amusing and laughter and want no longer spend the day buried in morose self-mirrored photo immersing themselves in the guilt of sin.

Erasmus and Hans Holbein had been buddies, and Erasmus had Hans Holbein illustrate his satirical essay, In Praise of Folly. They have been not exceptional intended as amusing, however insightful. For instance: When I honestly have a bit coins, I buy books; and if I definitely have any left, I buy meals, and garments, or In the land of the blind, the only-eyed man is king!

Holbein's illustrations for that text can without a problem be in evaluation to cartoons, in in recent times's meaning of the term. Holbein venerated Erasmus via the use of painting a portrait of him.

Dance of Death

As cited earlier, the Northern Renaissance artists often created woodblock printing.

Woodblock print is ready as a comfort. The artisan cuts away regions that aren't to expose at the paper. Those areas continue to be white at the same time as the flat areas include ink. They furthermore want to be reduce as a reflect picture, that is from right to left, due to the fact the final can be seen from left to proper. Many of Holbein's woodcuts were miniatures and his art work is exquisite in that regard. Many have been no massive than postage stamps.

This woodcut is a chain of movement scenes depicting the lives of thirty-4 people from numerous commands of society. Even a pope is pictured. Each woodblock confirmed a collection of people in the method of committing evil deeds and lack of lifestyles have become validated as a skeleton tormenting the humans in numerous methods.

The skeleton—Death—lances a knight in his belly; an obese glutton is being dragged out of her mattress. Death takes out his revenge on the determine of a lousy man who modified into wrongfully imprisoned. One of the functions of the piece is the complaint of the abusive clergy, as there are portrayals of an abbess being towed away through manner of Death and a fats abbot suffering the same destiny.

The Iconoclastic Riots

When the Protestant Reformation have become at its pinnacle inside the overdue 14th Century, there arose a notion inside these new Protestant sects that statues and religious representations had been idolatrous.

That is, it became felt that humans were worshipping the pics themselves. Its advocates had been keen on reciting the

Biblical tale approximately how the Israeli's were worshipping a golden calf at the foot of Mount Sinai. Hence, organisation of iconoclastic protestors went approximately the us of the us doing away with non secular artwork, sculptures, and pics of Biblical scenes. These they placed in the metropolis squares, smashed them to quantities and burnt them.

In that surroundings, Holbein have become now not able to locate commissioned paintings because of the religious symbolism of his art work. Erasmus then endorsed that Holbein go away Germany and Switzerland in which he lived and go to England. Erasmus furnished him with a letter of creation which he carried to Sir Thomas More.

More come to be the Chancellor to King Henry VIII, and he hostile the Protestant Reformation. Holbein settled there in 1532, and painted photos of dignitaries and royalty. Not most effective that, however he cherished portray buyers at their respective trades. His painting confirmed no longer simplest the people, however the system in their trades and become instructive to historians from that mindset.

Holbein used a wet-on-wet method to his oils which supplied possibilities for highlights and gently descending shading, giving the figures curvature and form. Imperfections, alongside aspect those because of injuries or damage have been delicately disguised. Henry's shoulders are sturdy and massive to provide the have an effect on of musculature and strength. Henry VIII come to be going to marry Anne Boleyn when that portray became achieved.

Perhaps the most famous of Holbein's masterpieces, finished in 1533, is The Ambassadors. One of the ambassadors he painted at Bridewell Palace come to be John De Danfield, the French ambassador to England. The exceptional ambassador modified into Grorbes de Selve, the bishop of Levaur. As he desired to link a photograph with the gadgets in use at a few diploma inside the Renaissance, the paining is replete with many of them. On the pinnacle shelf of a cabinet within the again of the figures, there's a celestial globe showing the heavenly our our bodies. The decrease shelf displays objects having to do with earth: a terrestrial globe, an oval compass, a cylindrical dial for figuring out the time of the day, a lyre with a string damaged, and a Lutheran hymnbook. Critics had interpreted that as which means that the ones were "damaged" times—torn by way of the use of way of the tumult of the numerous spiritual frenzies that characterized that thing. He moreover painted a material with a distorted skeleton on it symbolizing mortality.

As an expression of what was human, portraiture have grow to be vital, mainly because it become a manner of education people and immortalizing their photos all of the time.

Hans Holbein become invited to England to render the images of the Tudor Family. Henry VIII, of route, become the most first-rate. Holbein painted a large portrait of him across the twelve months 1538. Instead of depending upon backgrounds to set the mood, Holbein had a knack for conveying a mood with royalty implied through manner of the human expression in desire to symbolized via the usage of accoutrements which embody swords or scabbard and garb on my own. Backgrounds have been subdued, in order no longer to crush the easy import of the image itself.

## Chapter 12: Architects And Engineers

Like the severa Renaissance artists, Brunelleschi became born and raised in Florence. Although he have come to be a masterful architect, Filippo Brunselleschi (1377-1446) began out as a goldsmith, most of his life's artwork become architectural.

Brunelleschi's first primary commission changed into the Ospedale degli Innocenti of Hospital of the Innocents. Rather than using pointed arches, he implemented semi-spherical arches. They are smooth in layout and in fact uniform. Reliefs of toddlers are encircled like trademarks referred to as "tondi" in opposition to a blue background. The style is similar to the classical Romanesque fashion. Grey stone is contrasted with white. The proportions are unique and the complete constructing has been nicely-favored through artists for its thoughts-set.

The way for building the Dome of Santa Maria del Fiore still stays enormously of a thriller in recent times. Normally, the architects built their domes as a 1/2 of circle. Brunelleschi have become tasked with constructing a taller dome, and one with 8 aspects. When the layout modified into analyzed, it have end up located there has been no absolute center to the bottom of the dome. It changed into vague.

To make the dome taller than the conventional, Brunelleschi constructed edges to an octagonal base, the internal one being thicker than the alternative. Three other octagonal rings of stone and wood were constructed next. The motive of the jewelry have come to be like that of ribs on a barrel, and supposed to hold the dome from developing outward. To area the quantities of the jewelry in location, he devised a hoisting tool to elevate the bricks into region, the usage of pulleys, gears, and pressure-shafts. It is stated he may additionally moreover moreover have used ropes and hoisted each brick into region. As he left no written instructions or diagram, it's far however a mystery in recent times.

This dome is the heaviest and largest masonry dome ever built. There have become no vital wood or iron shape used to location the bricks. The indoors of the dome have become painted through none aside from Michelangelo's colleague and present day biographer, Giogio Vasari. The problems are from Dante's Divine Comedy. It took nearly twenty years to construct!

To that, a modest cupola changed into erected for the top and a translucent gold globe net sites on it to offer daytime into the otherwise dark indoors of the dome. Brunelleschi is likewise credited with developing one-trouble linear attitude, and his diagrams seem in lots of reference paintings books these days.

Devices of Interest

Brunelleschi invented a medieval fashion of hydraulic gadget, which he often used to beautify or hoist his stones into area. Through an complicated device of pulleys and gears, he designed the inner workings of transferring large curtains and characters during non secular plays. Angels flew thru the air causing terrific gasps at the part of the audiences. Although it have come to be pretty commonplace nowadays, Brunelleschi implemented pyrotechnics. There were explosions and fireworks of all types used to illustrate war scenes. They have been drastically implemented on celebratory activities.

In the early 15th Century, wars took place between the severa provinces of Italy.

Fortifications have been desired for Pisa and Siena. Not handiest turn out to be Brunelleschi recruited for such task but Michelangelo himself have become commissioned to art work on some for the province of Florence.

The nave of the Basilica of Santo Spirito became designed thru Brunelleschi. It is an energetic line of columns completed in Pietra Serena—a sandstone that is of a moderate green coloring, and moldings have been of Pietra Serena.

It is a form created through the use of manner of heating the stone internal molds and left to dry. Michelangelo imitated Brunelleschi's deign while he deliberate the Laurentian Library for the Medici own family. The constructing is completed within the shape of a go along with the dome ascending from the center of the flow centerpiece. He constructed his styles on squares and circles. The complete deign is geometrically appealing.

Filippo Brunelleschi died on the age of sixty-eight in 1446 in his appreciated Florence. He become buried inside the crypt at Santa Maria del Fiore which includes his dome—a fitting memorial to his reminiscence.

## Chapter 13: Writer And Architect
Leon Battista Alberti

Leon Battista Alberti (1404-1472) considered mathematics as a basis for shape. What prominent Alberti above so loads of his contemporaries was his attention of lighting.

The awesome studio designers of nowadays appearance upon lighting fixtures as a device in telling a tale, silently however successfully drawing the eyes of the traffic to the primary situation in their average performance.

Unlike precise artists during the Renaissance, he joined the clergy. And, in contrast to his contemporary-day, Brunelleschi, Alberti repeated the designs of the classical Greek and Roman structure. Therefore, he didn't shy away from the usage of the Ionic and Corinthian columns in his houses. Alberti modified into so enamored with the splendor of appropriate shape that he may want to emerge as so absorbed inside the seen enchantment of his paintings in place of the practicality.

When the Medici own family changed into ejected from Florence due to their tyrannical control of the republic, artists like Alberti had to voluntarily leave for a year from 1433 to 1434. Alberti modified into very well-known and related to the aristocracy of the period. Like severa his contemporaries, he come to be capable of find out safe haven in the Papal States.

Alberti become mentioned for his athletic prowess, even though testimonies approximately his capability have been appreciably exaggerated. He did, however, enjoy taming horses and mountain-climbing.

One of his maximum ordinary customers have end up Giocanni di Palolo Rucellai, a very rich noble. Rucellai's riches got here from banking in addition to the wool and dye trades, for which Florence grow to be famous within the 15th Century. For the Florentine, recognition become described with the useful useful resource of dress. The Rucellai circle of relatives discovered the manner to apply a pink dye called "Orsella rosso." It is made from lichens and located along the Mediterranean. One may want to make a fortune the use of this treasured dye.

Alberti's most mentioned architectural triumph come to be the Palazzo Rucellai in Florence. He used the not unusual Renaissance approach of utilising pilasters for constructing exteriors and interior partitions. A "pilaster" is a recessed column carved right proper right into a wall or façade. It delivered a decorative function to an otherwise monotonous wall. Within each phase he designed arched Gothic-styled domestic domestic home windows, which includes majesty and splendor.

Rucellai moreover commissioned Alberti to format the Santo Maria Novella, which become a church containing the remains of Rucellai's circle of relatives and those of different nobles. The maximum unusual feature approximately this constructing became the use of "serpentino," a inexperienced marble lessen in Prato, Italy. Alberti favored variety in his facades—and the serpentine made that constructing stand happy with others.

Each of the chapels inner have been precise to contain the remains of numerous noble households. On occasion, now not all crypts inside contained human stays, after which have been intended instead as memorials. The chapels had been designed in the shape of manner as to house frescoes of modern-day-day painters and stained glass home home windows.

Sometimes frescoes of this era no longer quality had portrayals of the Christian saints, but human beings of the households whom they have been devoted to. One of the chapels—the Capella Strozzi de Mantova—has representations taken from Dante's Divine Comedy. While Alberti rendered the outside and fashionable architectural format, the chapels had been commissioned one after the alternative.

www.ingramcontent.com/pod-product-compliance
Lightning Source LLC
Chambersburg PA
CBHW070555010526
44118CB00012B/1324